11808

11808

Agee

HIS LIFE REMEMBERED

Edited by Ross Spears and Jude Cassidy
With a Narrative by Robert Coles

Holt, Rinehart and Winston
New York

Published by Holt, Rinehart and Winston, 383 Madison Avenue,
New York, New York 10017.
Published simultaneously in Canada by Holt, Rinehart and
Winston of Canada, Limited.

Library of Congress Cataloging in Publication Data
Main entry under title:
Agee.
Bibliography: p.
Includes the words and pictures from the documentary
film, Agee, as well as excerpts from James Agee's own
writings.
1. Agee, James, 1909–1955.   2. Authors, American—
20th century—Biography.   I. Agee, James, 1909–1955.
II. Spears, Ross.   III. Cassidy, Jude.   IV. Coles,
Robert.   V. Agee (Motion picture)
PS3501.G35Z55   1985   813'.52 {B}   84-19776
ISBN 0-03-060099-0

First Edition

Designed by Lucy Albanese
Printed in the United States of America
1 3 5 7 9 10 8 6 4 2

ISBN 0-03-060099-0

For Mary Spears and Father Flye

Contents

Preface

James Agee became my favorite writer in the summer of 1968 after my third year of college, when I chanced upon *Let Us Now Praise Famous Men*, Agee's well-known account of three tenant families in rural Alabama during the Depression. The writing was superb; the subject matter compelling. But it was Agee's ethical and artistic struggle that lifted the work to a special place in my life and, I believe, to a unique place in American literature. Quite simply, *Famous Men* is the record of a young man out to change the world with words.

Beethoven said a thing as rash and noble as the best of his work. By my memory, he said: "He who understands my music can never know unhappiness again." I believe it. And I would be a liar and a coward and one of your safe world if I should fear to say the same words of my best perception, and of my best intention.

In the late 1960s, when the struggles for peace and for equality in the United States were part of daily, even hourly, conversation, these words had enormous resonance in my life. Agee's love for the families in Alabama was radical, and his attempt to communicate their lives was tireless. *Let Us Now Praise Famous Men* overwhelmed me, which I am sure was Agee's intention. I reread the book several times. I wrote long college papers about it. I read the rest of Agee's work—his novels, his short prose, his film criticism, his scripts, his poetry, and with each work my early enthusiasm was confirmed and strengthened. Eventually I began to feel the necessity to form some kind of response.

In 1974 Jude Cassidy and I began what our initial sponsors, the Tennessee Arts Commission, thought would be a Bicentennial film on the life of James Agee, who had been born in Knoxville and had spent his early life in Tennessee. The film, entitled *Agee*, took five years to complete. We had very little money to work with and very little knowledge of where to get more, but we kept plugging away—writing letters, collecting still photographs, doing odd jobs, and shooting film when we managed to raise money. When we became discouraged from time to time, a glance into *Let Us Now Praise Famous Men* usually put our problems into perspective.

By far the most enjoyable parts of the filmmaking process were the encounters with the significant people and places in Agee's life, and it is the filmed result of these encounters that gives the film its power. We shot as much of the film as possible in the places where Agee lived and worked. We filmed excerpts from *A Death in the Family* in Agee's childhood neighborhood in Knoxville and scenes from *The Morning Watch* at St. Andrew's School in Tennessee. We filmed members of the sharecropper families from *Famous Men* for several weeks in Hale County, Alabama. We interviewed Robert Fitzgerald in the library of Agee's Harvard dormitory, and we filmed Mia Agee in the house in which she and Agee had lived in Greenwich Village. We filmed, but did not use, scenes at several other Agee residences—Phillips Exeter Academy; Monk's Farm, New Jersey; Malibu, California; and Hillsdale, New York. Each of these experiences was precious to us and important to the film.

Agee was completed in 1979 and was very well received. It won a Blue Ribbon at the American Film Festival, and it became the first filmed literary biography to receive an Academy Award nomination. This book is based on interviews that were conducted during the making of the film. We were unable to include several of the interview segments in the ninety-minute film, and they are offered here for the first time. All of the interviews are presented as they were spoken, with a minimal amount of editing. The long essay by Robert Coles was written especially for this book.

There have been two particularly gratifying kinds of responses to the film. The first is when a close friend of James Agee, after seeing the film, comes up to one of us and says, "Yes, I knew Jim, and that's the way he was." That has happened several times. The second and much more frequent response is when a member of the audience asks after a screening, "Which Agee work do you think I should read first?" We hope this book will have the same effect.

Ross Spears
New York, 1985

Acknowledgments

The film *Agee* could not have been made without the help of a great many people, and we are grateful for the opportunity to acknowledge them. First of all we thank the friends of James Agee who gave their time and energy to be in the film: Mia Agee, Father James Harold Flye, Dwight Macdonald, Robert Saudek, Olivia Wood, Robert Fitzgerald, Alma Neuman, John Huston, Elizabeth Tingle, Ellie Mae Burroughs, and President Jimmy Carter. For conversations and advice we are grateful to Harvey Simmonds, David McDowell, and Erik Wensberg; for still photographs, Helen Levitt, David Herwaldt, Donald Dietz, Olivia Wood, Mia Agee, Paula Tyler, and the estates of Florence Homolka and Walker Evans. We also thank the composer, Kenton Coe; the cameraman, Anthony Forma; the actor,

Earl McCarroll; and a dedicated crew: John and Diane Jennings, Peter Rosenberg, Jay Goldman, Jim Gillie, Rick Blaine, and Ilo Milton.

For their support in Tennessee we thank Gordon Holl of the Tennessee Arts Commission: Mary Jane Coleman of the Sinking Creek Film Celebration; Barbara Silver, Jill McLean, Betty Swoyer, Nellie McNeil, Cam Crockett, Virginia and Sidney Smallwood, and John Roach of the James Agee Film Project; Lucille and James Spears; Marianne and Bill Henson, Lance Tacke, Dale Moore, Bill Daniels of the Epworth Ministry in Knoxville; and Father Franklin Martin of the St. Andrew's School in Monteagle, Tennessee.

In the construction of the book, the editorial assistance of Tracy Brown, Donald Hutter, and David Stanford has been invaluable. We are thankful for their help.

Lastly, we are enormously grateful for the support and patience of our families: Mary and Ross Spears, Jr., and Elsie and Lloyd Cooper.

Father James Harold Flye, an Episcopal priest, taught history at St. Andrew's School near Sewanee, Tennessee, from 1918 to 1954. Father Flye and James Agee developed a close relationship during the years Agee was a student at St. Andrew's (1919–22). This friendship, and a later correspondence, continued throughout Agee's life. A collection of Agee's letters to Father Flye, *The Letters of James Agee to Father Flye*, was published in 1962. He died in 1985 at the age of 100.

Paula Tyler was Agee's mother's younger sister. She was an accomplished musician and taught young James Agee to play the piano at the Agees' Knoxville home.

Oliver Hodge was a slightly older schoolmate of Agee at St. Andrew's School in Tennessee.

Robert Saudek was Agee's roommate at Harvard. He later produced television's "Omnibus" series and commissioned Agee to write the script for a five-part series on the life of Abraham Lincoln.

Olivia Saunders Wood and James Agee were married from 1933 until 1938. She was the daughter of Dr. Arthur Percy Saunders and Louise Saunders of Clinton, New York. She met Agee while both were attending classes at Harvard in 1930.

Dwight Macdonald, who preceded Agee at Phillips Exeter Academy by several years, received a letter from Agee in 1927 that marked the beginning of their lifelong friendship. For several years they were fellow writers at *Fortune* magazine. Macdonald went on to become one of the most respected literary figures of his generation, working as a critic, editor, translator, and frequent contributor to such magazines as *The New Yorker*, *The Nation*, *Partisan Review*, *The New Republic*, and *The New York Review of Books*. He died in 1982.

Robert Fitzgerald became friends with Agee during their years at Harvard where they shared an interest in poetry. They remained good friends in New York throughout the 1930s, and during 1940 and 1941 they worked together as book reviewers for *Time* magazine. Following Fitzgerald's move to Italy in the 1940s, they corresponded until Agee's death. Fitzgerald is best known for his poetry, as well as his recent translations of *The Iliad* and *The Odyssey*. He died in 1985.

Walker Evans was one of America's foremost still photographers. He and Agee became close friends in New York in the early 1930s. Together they spent two months in 1936 in Hale County, Alabama, gathering the material that became the book *Let Us Now Praise Famous Men*. His other works include *American Photographs* (1938), *Many Are Called* (1966), and *Walker Evans: First and Last* (1978). He died in 1975.

Elizabeth Tingle was nineteen years old when James Agee and Walker Evans traveled through Hale County, Alabama, on the project that became *Let Us Now Praise Famous Men*. She was the second eldest daughter of the Tingle family and is referred to in the book as Margaret Ricketts.

Ellie Mae Burroughs was a twenty-seven-year-old tenant farmer when *Let Us Now Praise Famous Men* was researched. Agee and Evans stayed at her home during part of their visit in Alabama. She is referred to as Allie Mae Gudger in the book.

Alma Mailman Neuman met James Agee while he was a student at Harvard. They attended parties at the home of Dr. Arthur and Louise Saunders in Clinton, New York, where they played music together. After their marriage in 1938, they lived in New Jersey, where Agee wrote *Let Us Now Praise Famous Men*, and then in New York until their separation in 1941. Their son, Joel Agee, was born in March 1940.

Mia Fritsch Agee was born in Vienna, Austria, and emigrated to the United States in 1933. She met James Agee when she was a researcher at *Fortune* magazine in 1939. They were married in 1944. Their three children are Teresa, born in 1946; Andrea, born in 1950; and John, born in 1954.

John Huston has been a well-known film director since his first film, *The Maltese Falcon*, in 1941. Huston and Agee became friends in the late 1940s and collaborated on the screenplay for *The African Queen*. Huston's many other films include *The Battle of San Pietro*, *The Treasure of the Sierra Madre*, *Fat City*, *Wise Blood*, *The Man Who Would Be King*, and *Under the Volcano*.

David McDowell attended St. Andrew's School a few years after Agee had left. Through Father Flye he made Agee's acquaintance and established a friendship that was to last for the extent of Agee's life. After attending Kenyon College, he worked as an editor and founded McDowell, Obolensky, Inc., the publishers of *A Death in the Family*. He served as the executor of the James Agee Trust until his death in 1985.

Part 1

All My People

are larger bodies than mine, quiet, with voices gentle and mean-
ingless like the voices of sleeping birds. One is an artist, he is
living at home. One is a musician, she is living at home. One
is my mother who is good to me. One is my father who is good
to me. By some chance, here they are, all on this earth; and
who shall ever tell the sorrow of being on this earth, lying, on
quilts, on the grass, in a summer evening, among the sounds
of night. —from *A Death in the Family*

*S*ome writers, among them James Agee, most certainly, make
of their lives compelling dramatic presentations—companion pieces to
what they have written. We readers end up contemplating not only
essays, poems, stories, but the way a particular writer chose to spend
his or her time on this earth. Sometimes, as in Agee's case, the life
becomes a legend, shadowing or even thoroughly overshadowing even
a significant body of literary work. A great amount of criticism has
been devoted to examining the Agee legend: Agee the hard-living
romantic, whose excesses drastically foreshortened his life and thwarted
a potentially brilliant writing career; Agee the dedicated and quite
idiosyncratic individual, whose artistic gifts were expressed according
to his own peculiar momentum, and whose works ought to be judged

on their own merits, rather than according to someone's self-righteous (envious? straitlaced? academic?) notions of what they should have been.

He was born in Knoxville, Tennessee, on November 27, 1909. His family background was mixed, socially. His mother, Laura, was the daughter of Joel Tyler, who owned a machine company (Agee's father, Hugh James Agee, known as "Jay," later worked there). On his mother's side were to be found artists, musicians, successful businessmen. Jay was of rural Appalachian ancestry, but not, as has been sometimes averred, back-hollow stock. His grandfather had been a physician and well-known politician. His father, Henry Clay Agee, taught school in Campbell County, Tennessee. So did Jay for a while, but he left the countryside for Knoxville, where he took a job in the post office. In 1906 he was transferred to, of all places, Cristobal, Panama—the Canal Zone at the time was a distinctly American address—and he and his bride enjoyed living abroad. Two years later the couple was back in Tennessee. After a brief stint with the Louisville and Nashville Railroad, Jay and Laura moved to Knoxville, where the birth of a son, James Rufus, then a daughter, Emma, gave additional strength to their relationship. It was apparently a union of opposites: the shy, deeply religious, quite refined and cultivated wife, and the hearty, outgoing husband. But on May 18, 1916, the marriage ended abruptly and tragically when Jay Agee was killed in an automobile accident. The sudden loss of his father was a major event in the life of James Agee, then six.

We know of that death, of course, as readers of *A Death in the Family*, published shortly after James Agee's own tragic death on May 16, 1955. Though a novel, the book is heavily autobiographical, the boy sharing Agee's own childhood nickname of "Rufus," and the circumstances of the death matching those of Agee's own father.

James Agee's early years, the splits and tensions of his family life, were constantly on his mind. As a writer, he labored long and hard to capture the light and darkness of his own specific childhood, but he also saw and passionately attempted, as an artist, to represent through the telling the universals of human experience, the strangeness of life, its deep complexity and constant unpredictability. In "Knoxville 1915," a prelude of sorts to *A Death in the Family*, a boy has his reverie, observes that those around him, his parents, his relatives, have "larger bodies" than he does, and are "quiet, with voices gentle and meaningless like the voices of sleeping birds." He proceeds with an enumeration of some of those grown-ups, then remarks that "by some chance, here they are, all on this earth."

I have taught James Agee's writings for many years, and often students stop at that sentence, want to know whether a boy of six or under would likely entertain such a thought, in the tradition of stoic resignation. Other students, invariably, remind us that we are reading, after all, a *novel*, no matter the personal references one may decipher without great difficulty. I suspect Agee had little interest in exaggerating or distorting the possibilities of childhood, his or anyone else's. He was an exceptionally interested and keen observer of children; at one point he worked with a photographer and filmmaker, Helen Levitt, who had a similar desire to do justice to the ways boys and girls look and act. He drew upon his own life—as what writer explicitly or implicitly doesn't?—as part of an ambitious attempt at approximating the truth of early life. The very first poem, in *Permit Me Voyage*, a verse collection that won publication for a quite young James Agee in the Yale Younger Poets Series, goes like this

Child, should any pleasant boy
Find you lovely, many could,
Wind not up between your joy
The sly delays of maidenhood:
Spread all your beauty in his sight
And do him kindness every way,
Since soon, too soon, the wolfer night
Climbs in between, and ends fair play.

A conventional piece of sentimentality, and today, on obvious grounds, a thoroughly arguable bit of advice, no matter the speaker's interest in bitter and gloomy irony, rather than libertine exhortation or manipulation. The point is a writer's continuing attention to the early years of life—the sense that there is, therein, mystery and magic and truth, to be discovered and brought entertainingly to the attention of others. It would be foolish to suggest that this interest was a consequence of Agee's father's death, but certainly his early years were deeply affected by it.

Among the writers Agee admired, Hart Crane figured prominently. Maybe that poet's words offer enough helpful psychobiographical background for an understanding of the first part of Agee's life:

> *And so it was I entered the broken world*
> *To trace the visionary company of love, its voice*
> *An instance in the wind (I know not whither hurled)*
> *But not for long to hold each desperate choice.*

No question that the death of his father meant a "broken world" for James Agee. In 1919 his mother took the children with her to live at St. Andrew's School near Sewanee, Tennessee, where Agee became a student. It was, and still is, an Episcopal school founded by the Order of the Holy Cross. Mrs. Agee knew her son was bright, inquisitive, active, quick-thinking. She wanted him to get a strong religious education, but also a superior academic one. Not least, she wanted him, fatherless, to be near grown men of high character. Agee lived at St. Andrew's between the ages of ten and fourteen—and the experience nourished a later story, a novella, *The Morning Watch*, published first in *Botteghe Oscure* (1950). That long story offers yet another evocation of early adolescence, the continuing tension between eagerly embraced idealism and the newly pressing demands of the flesh. Agee played off the awesome significance and solemnity of Easter week against the prankish liveliness and exuberant egoism of the youths in a religious boarding school. Again, however, it is risky to assume Agee's writing can be seen as a directly autobiographical account of his own experiences. He used everything he had in him, and then, still hungry for stimulation, roamed far and wide to absorb sights, sounds, words, and deeds. He was a storyteller. He drew on autobiography all right, giving it the shape and texture of fiction, but he was also a journalist, ever responsive to the stimulation of events in the larger world.

At St. Andrew's he met Father James Harold Flye, a teacher and an amateur photographer of some distinction. Father Flye was a kind and thoughtful man who quickly spotted the incipient virtues, intellectual and moral, of young Agee. Much of what we know of Agee came through the publication of his side of a correspondence he maintained with Father Flye, a correspondence that began when he was in high school and continued throughout his life. After Agee's death, an unposted letter to Father Flye was found on the living-room mantel in his Greenwich Village apartment. Theirs was a deep and abiding friendship. Clearly Father Flye became a father to Agee. Even in the 1940s, when he was a grown man and called Jim by everyone else, Agee continued to sign his letters to Father Flye "Rufus." Certainly Mrs. Agee's hope that her son would find fatherly companionship at St. Andrew's School was fulfilled. But Father Flye, now in his late nineties and still very much with us, has many impressive qualities, and they ought not be ignored in favor of the descriptive word *fatherly*.

In a way, I suppose, Flye combined aspects of both sides of Agee's family background: the mother's artistic, literary, and religious interests, and the father's wonderful loving kindness and interest in teaching. These two exquisitely sensitive souls were well matched and became good, good friends. The young Agee traveling abroad with the solicitous and knowing Father Flye was, admittedly, glad to be a son of sorts. And Flye, a man who was married but had no children, was certainly glad to be something of a father. But the older Agee, in his letters, was also simply grateful to have a person of truly kindred spirit on this earth: familiar, responsive, attentive, comprehending—they had the kind of friendship that becomes steadying, a reference point, like firm ground underfoot.

In 1925, during the summer, the boy and his teacher-priest-friend toured England and France. In the autumn of that year young Agee, not yet sixteen, entered Phillips Exeter Academy, located in southern New Hampshire, one of this country's most intellectually demanding private schools. In the spring of 1981 I had the privilege of being at Exeter with Father Flye and Erik Wensberg, who was working hard on what I know will be an important and discerning biography of Agee. The school was commemorating its distinguished alumnus with a symposium. I asked Father Flye how (as he saw it back then) Agee had managed as an Exeter student. The reply was a model of suggestive, tactful brevity: "I think he must have *struggled* through the school, as he did through life! He was bright, of course; but he was never the conventional student. I can imagine some teachers thoroughly puzzled by this tall, lanky fellow from the highlands of Tennessee, with a mind of his own, great gifts, and a determination to use them as he saw fit!"

We do know that at Exeter Agee was both a promising writer, a good actor, a first-rate student in English and Latin, and a very poor student in geometry and chemistry, both of which he failed in his senior year. He won English prizes. He became an associate editor, then editor-in-chief, of the *Phillips Exeter Monthly Magazine*. He was, even then, taken both with writers of the past (a voracious reader) and the present (ever eager to hear and meet the likes of Booth Tarkington and Sinclair Lewis). Without question it was at Exeter that Agee the writer was born. Father Flye did not recall his young friend being so inclined at St. Andrew's School. At Exeter Agee began corresponding with the essayist and critic Dwight Macdonald, who had preceded him there by several years. Macdonald gives their alma mater a measure of credit for Agee's early choice of career: "Exeter was the place for writers. It had a marvelous English Department."

The quality of that department was affirmed by its students. In May 1928, for example, an eighteen-year-old Agee published in the *Exeter Monthly* a long (500 lines) poem, "Ann Garner," which was later included in his book *Permit Me Voyage*. The poem begins:

> *Like a stone set to mark a death, the bed*
> *leaned through the leaping darkness, gaunt and square*
> *Against the firelight. In her agony*
> *Bent like a birch ice-laden, Ann Garner lay:*
> *The silent woman by her in the dimness*
> *Turned to the firelight, and said to her husband*
> *"She's laborin' hard; best set the plow beneath her."*

The poem is a narrative drama—a youthful statement in the romantic tradition. Agee, at the time he wrote it, was much taken with

Walt Whitman, though he later changed his opinion. But "Ann Garner" showed a part of Agee that stayed with him to the end—a preoccupation with life's dramatic moments, with the sources of our energy, our achievements, our failures. The central figure, for whom the poem is named, is a vital, nourishing person, yet gives birth to a stillborn child. Agee never lost his precocious preoccupation with ambiguity and irony. He appreciated (too much, some would argue) and portrayed the inconsistencies and contradictions that are part of everyone's makeup—even those who strain hard in their theoretical thinking for a critical uniformity and logic. Agee's interest in subjectivity, in the unpredictable and stubborn variations of our emotional experiences, informed everything he wrote.

Down to Cambridge, to Harvard, he went in the autumn of 1928—no unusual trek. But once in those Victorian college buildings, once a part of the Yard, he quickly established himself as different, if not peculiar. He kept irregular hours, a habit he then maintained throughout his adult life: long, alert, working or pleasure-filled nights and short sleeping sessions carried out in the morning. He gravitated quickly to literature courses, to the college's writing circles, and to the movies, especially Westerns. One classmate and friend remembers him as "Byronic." Another, Robert Fitzgerald, described him this way: "The figure in the front row on my right, looming and brooding and clutching his book, his voice very low, almost inaudible but deliberate and distinct, as though ground there by great interior pressure." In a single sentence Fitzgerald captures Agee's primary attributes: "Here, in the front row, were shyness and power and imagination."

At Harvard he developed habits and interests that lasted the rest of his life. He set his own priorities, rebelled against those of others, drank immoderately upon certain occasions, and, as mentioned, thought nothing of turning night into day, and vice versa. He became, actually, a fiercely independent, iconoclastic, rule-breaking writer—talented, energetic, and marvelously observant. By 1931, he was president of the *Harvard Advocate*. He'd also had a taste of academic probation.

Agee both loved and despised Cambridge. He loved the fine literary and philosophical minds he met there, but despised the smugness and self-importance that also reside there. One summer (between his freshman and sophomore years) he went west and harvested wheat in Nebraska and Kansas. It was just the job for him—the American wanderer, the yeoman, the poet building his muscles, sleeping under the big, mid-continent sky, free from the stale air of academic life. But he came back gladly in the fall, and his mind continued to grow. The tension between the attraction of intense and intellectual places like Cambridge or Greenwich Village and that of the supposedly simpler and less affected ways of the South, the West, and the New England countryside, vibrated within him throughout his life. The same tension was there in the complicated attitudes he held toward the literary and intellectual world to which he belonged, but which he also scorned.

At Harvard Agee met Olivia Saunders, who, from 1933 to 1938, would be his first wife. They took I. A. Richards's class together, and often went to the home of Olivia's parents in Clinton, New York. Her father, a chemistry professor, was an accomplished musician and a friend of Richards, and of Alexander Woollcott as well. Agee was a great favorite of these older writers—the extremely talented and promising Harvardian and, too, the wonderfully exuberant, funny, convivial fellow guest.

In his senior year at Harvard, Agee and some of his *Advocate* friends did a brilliant parody of *Time*, which was then only a few years old. One of Agee's best friends, Dwight Macdonald, was by then actually working on a different Luce magazine, *Fortune*. Agee did not exactly have the best prospects when he graduated in 1932. The Depression had a firm grip on the economy. The *Time* parody probably helped Macdonald get him a job at *Fortune*. With this fortuitous break a journalistic career of almost two decades was launched.

In 1933 Agee was a New Yorker, a resident of Manhattan. He worked in a new skyscraper, the Chrysler Building, on the fifty-second floor. His habits as a *Fortune* essayist have become a part of the Agee legend: Agee and his Beethoven symphonies blasting away through the night, the lighted streets of the world's greatest city far below. Agee and coffee, Agee and booze, Agee and the typewriter, Agee and cigarettes, and most important, Agee and deadlines—which seemed to take on, with him, a literal meaning. He drove himself ruthlessly and experienced terrible spells of apprehension and despair as he contested time and his superiors, not to mention his own exacting conscience, in a (usually) desperate effort to turn in finished copy before it was too late.

But for all the drama, if not histrionics, the articles, by and large, got done; and invariably they were brilliantly constructed, witty, informative, entertaining. Here was a poet harnessed to the commercial world and somehow able to sing (well, indeed) for his supper. He wrote of rugs and roads and railroads. He wrote of flowers and towns and quinine cartels and commodities speculators. He was able to mobilize within himself the dispassionate curiosity of the reporter, and when linked to the storyteller's eye for detail, the result was superb journalistic narrative. Just below the surface was a strong moral sensibility, held in check by the constraints of the Luce empire, but never banished outright—even when the subject was as innocuous as strawberries: "In England, behind walls of a respectable age, strawberries are still served at Solemn High Tea. In England this June the school tuck-shop will be clamorous with hard-hatted little Harrovians absorbing 'dringers,' a somewhat lily-gilding mixture of fresh strawberries and strawberry ice cream."

This excerpt was served to me in an English course I took at college, when Agee was a name I was yet to know. We were told, as Agee may have told himself, that any crop, fruit or vegetable or cereal or so-called raw material, can be used to open up whatever doors the writer wishes. Strawberries took Agee to the privileged realms of England's so-called public schools—an indirect reminder to *Fortune*'s wealthy that while millions could take no meal, however meager, for granted, a small group of kids, vain and arrogant, were making an innocent strawberry an object of scandal.

In 1936 Agee, along with photographer Walker Evans, was sent to Alabama to write about cotton, the staple crop of the sharecropper and tenant farm agriculture in the South. This assignment took Agee through a long and memorable personal and moral struggle and eventually resulted in a book, *Let Us Now Praise Famous Men*, which is Agee's single most significant piece of writing.

Nineteen thirty-six was an election year, and in the small farming community Agee chose to study (between Montgomery and Birmingham) the Depression had become a way of life. Strong federal efforts by the Roosevelt administration had softened considerably the sharpest edges of extreme poverty and unemployment, but the country's economic system, everyone agreed, was still quite sick. Few were in worse shape than the South's farmers, both black and white. At the time *Fortune* was not interested in doing an article on rural black people. For that matter, Agee and Evans were not sent down to do a searching documentary of the wretched circumstances bedeviling white share-croppers either. Cotton was still king, and an economic analysis of that royal crop, colorfully written, was what Agee's bosses had in mind.

For Agee, however, this was an opportunity of the greatest import: a way of drawing upon interests he'd had since his southern boyhood and of exploring not only an economic problem, but the moral aspects of a nation's life. It was also a way of escaping Manhattan's cosmopolitan culture in pursuit of that elusive honesty, purity, integrity so many of us keep looking for around corner after corner of our lives. And he was to work with Walker Evans, a friend of similarly conflicted temperament, who was eager to pursue Art, willing to break rules to do so, stubbornly independent, of broad sensibility, and not beyond calling upon the bourbon as a dear, helpful friend.

They stayed in Alabama more than a month, through July and into August. They lived with three families and tried to understand deeply and respectfully their everyday existence. In the end they failed their working mission; *Fortune* never would show its readers, through Agee's words and Evans's photographs, the human side of cotton production. Evans saw beauty as well as pain, and both were within his grasp. His pictures show terribly hurt, perplexed, and vulnerable men, women, children, and scenes, interior and exterior, considered with an artist's concentration.

Evans and Agee in the South were two well-bred and well-educated young men in search of careers in the arts. There was not much time for them to figure out, in detail, what their ultimate purposes were. They were guests. Their task was to keep up with the daily rhythms of their subjects—extremely harassed people, living penniless under a hot sun with no great expectation of doing very well in the world.

Agee was as hungry in his own way as his hosts, as confused and uncertain and apprehensive as they. They were up at dawn and ready for bed shortly after sundown—tired from hard, demanding agricultural labor. He was up with them, trying to learn the details of their work, their ways—driven, one realizes, by a strong conscience determined, this time, to have its say, and then some. The seething, anarchic re-belliousness that had hitherto (at Exeter and Harvard, and in Manhat-tan) taken an erratic course, now apparent in sarcasm or satire or parody, now buried under layers of religious sentiment or literary analysis, began at last to emerge as a full-fledged moral force. It was as if Agee had heard a voice within saying, loud and clear: "Here you are, close to the proud and hurt Appalachian people of your childhood, close to the people your Lord Jesus Christ kept mentioning, the ones he kept near at hand, attempting to heal and feed and comfort. You had best take exceeding care, you who are good with words, you who have been quick to turn on others, the hypocrites and pretenders and sycophants, the self-absorbed tastemakers of a world very far, socially and culturally, from north-central Alabama."

◆　　◆　　◆

Father Flye

I don't know if I can make very much of a description. I would say I like children, and certainly those that are intelligent and interesting and can talk can make very charming companions. And this was the case with Jim.

He was raised in the home of his grandfather, whose name was Joel Tyler, and that would mean classics and literature; and they knew a fair amount about music. They were not upper-class financially, but they were cultivated people and of fine quality. Mr. and Mrs. Tyler were both graduates of the University of Michigan at Ann Arbor, and I think Mrs. Tyler was one of the first women to get a degree there. Jim's mother was born in Michigan, she and her twin brother, Hugh. And when these two children were five or six years old, the father, partly on account of the climate in that frigid region in Michigan, came down to Tennessee, to Knoxville, and invested in some timberland that he heard there was plenty of around here.

Mr. Tyler, Jim's grandfather, was an extremely independent person in his thought and opinions—the old American tradition of personal independence. This is where he stood and he wasn't modifying it for anybody. He wanted to stand on his own feet and pay his own way and not take any favors. In religion he'd be what they used to call a "free-thinker," or, we'd say, an agnostic. You would hardly say anti-religious, or certainly not a dogmatic atheist, but he felt, "Well, I don't know. If you see something there, I'm glad you do; but I can't see it." His wife belonged to the Unitarians once, and that isn't anything very dogmatic, I must say.

Jim's father's people were quite different from the Tylers. They were not illiterate, to be sure, but they weren't of that kind of background. They were from that East Tennessee region up around Knoxville-LaFollette, I think. They were small-town and country people, back for three or four generations there. They'd come down from Virginia into Tennessee.

James Rufus Agee and his mother, Laura Tyler Agee, 1911. This photograph was printed on a postcard. Message on back: "For dear 'Grabbie' with my love. I was feeling like a fight, but this is 'me.' Your grandson, Rufus, 19 mos."

James Agee, his sister, Emma, and his mother, Laura, 1912.

The Agee house on Highland Avenue, Knoxville, Tennessee.

Clockwise from left: *Joel Tyler, Agee's grandfather; Emma Tyler, Agee's grandmother; Hugh Tyler, Agee's uncle; Laura Tyler Agee, Agee's mother; James Agee; and Emma Agee, Agee's sister, Knoxville, 1916. (Photo courtesy Paula Tyler)*

Laura Tyler Agee and Emma Tyler, Agee's mother and grandmother, Knoxville, 1916. (Photo courtesy Paula Tyler)

From left: *Hugh Tyler, Agee's uncle; Paula Tyler, Agee's aunt and Hugh's sister; and Emma Tyler. (Photo courtesy Paula Tyler)*

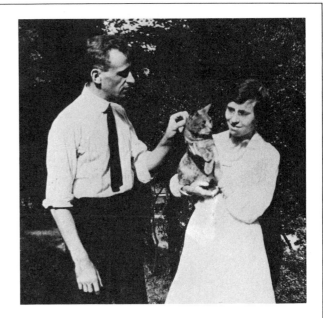

ABOVE: *Hugh Tyler and his younger sister, Paula Tyler, Knoxville, c. 1915.*

LEFT: *Hugh Tyler with unidentified woman, Knoxville, c. 1915.*

ABOVE: *Hugh Tyler with Agee's great-aunt, Jessie Tyler, an Anglo-Catholic nun, c. 1915.*

RIGHT: *Laura Tyler Agee and Emma Agee. Knoxville, c. 1915. (Photo courtesy Paula Tyler)*

Paula Tyler

Jay Agee, Jim's father, was very good-looking. Laura met him at dancing school, night dancing school. Sometimes I'd come home to our house, and we had high steps to the porch, and they'd be sitting on one of the porch steps talking. They were getting engaged. His father was a country schoolteacher. Jay didn't go to college, but he helped his brothers through college. He was very intellectual. He liked reading very much, and he'd educated himself really by what he'd done after he'd left school. Most of his career was with the United States Post Office, both in this country and in Panama when they were doing the Canal. They lived in the Canal Zone. When he came back, after some time and difficulty (he had had malaria), my father, Jay's father-in-law, gave him a job as a secretary in his office.

Father Flye

I remember Mr. Tyler saying to me once that Jim Agee's father needed college less than any man he had ever met.

Paula Tyler

I taught Rufus piano when he was little. He was terrifically musical. When he was trying to make up his mind what he was going to do in his life—I guess when he was going to Harvard, or perhaps before he went—I said, "Before you decide what you're going to do, don't forget that you could do wonders in music. You're very gifted." And he said, "Well, I think it's not hard enough for me. I want to do the writing."

A little boy up the street hadn't a bicycle and Rufus gave him his. Of course when the family heard about it, they thought they'd better do something. So I think Laura, his mother, went up and talked to the family and got it back. He didn't mind that either. I don't think he thought anything about it. It was a tricycle—whose was it?—it doesn't make any difference.

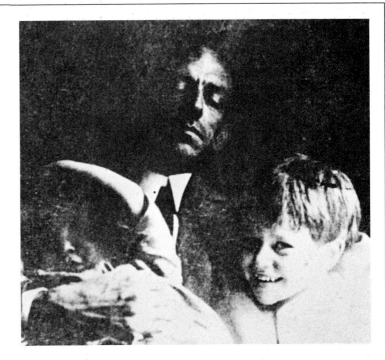

ABOVE: *Hugh James Agee (known as "Jay"), Agee's father, date unknown.*

RIGHT: *Hugh ("Jay") James Agee, with his children, Emma and James, 1912. (Photo courtesy Paula Tyler)*

FOUND DEAD ON CLINTON PIKE

James Agee, of This City, Pinned Under Automobile.

When Car Struck Embankment and Overturned Was Returning From LaFollette.

ABOVE: *Obituary of Hugh James Agee from* The Journal and Tribune, *Knoxville, Tennessee, 1916.*

RIGHT: Clockwise from left: *Laura Tyler Agee, Paula Tyler, Emma Tyler, James Agee, and Emma Agee. (Photo courtesy Paula Tyler)*

Father Flye

Jim's mother was deeply religious. And from two years after her husband's death she had spent the months of each academic year on the Cumberland Plateau in Tennessee, at St. Andrew's, a little community and school associated with a monastic order in the Episcopal Church.

In 1905 the Order of the Holy Cross had gone down to Tennessee, to a place two miles from Sewanee, and bought a little property, and had built a sort of priory down there in which some of the monks lived. And almost immediately they got some of the neighborhood boys in, who didn't have much opportunity for education, and began to teach them, and that was the foundation of St. Andrew's School.

The religious atmosphere was very strong. That is, the place was definitely founded as a Christian enterprise. There were classes in religious instruction. The boys went to chapel, and morning prayers, and evening prayers after supper, and the angelus was rung from the monastery bell. The holy days would be kept, and if there was any possible conflict between an academic and a religious observance, the religious came first. That is, when we were keeping a holy day and had to cut one of the classes, we did it.

The boys were encouraged to participate in religion to whatever degree their conscience would permit. Some of them had come from intensely Protestant backgrounds, like the Southern Baptists, and so on. I remember one of the boys speaking to me once, and he said, "I hadn't ever been in a Catholic church 'til I come here. And the first Sunday I didn't know what it was all about. I went in there to go to church, and I thought that, well, like I was used to, the preacher would come in and start rarin' and stampedin'." And instead of that he found this liturgical service with the High Mass sung, and the liturgical forms, and no "rarin' or stampedin' " at all.

The first year that I was there, there was this wide spread of, well, age for one thing. That is, they had very young boys there, some of them seven or eight years old, with a special dormitory for them and a matron, and from there on up. In that first year of my being there some boys came in who'd been overseas in the First World War. They'd come back for a little more education. And there was also a spread in mental ability.

*Chapel at St. Andrew's School, near Sewanee,
Tennessee. (Photo courtesy Paula Tyler)*

*Father James Harold Flye at St. Andrew's School.
(Photo courtesy Father James Harold Flye)*

Some boys were really uneducable; they just never could go further than the elements. And yet, that first year, I taught a class in Cicero, third-year Latin, and had some very good students in it.

None of the boys there had any money to speak of. They made the tuition and board very minimal, almost nothing, and the school couldn't have run except for gifts sent in by persons who were sympathetic with that sort of an education, the Christian auspices.

Oliver Hodge

Rufus was somewhat of a loner. In the first place, his mother occupied the old Stroup cottage near the grounds and he could take off for home, whereas we had nowhere to go but right there. Having a mother there probably led somewhat to his reputation as a momma's boy because he had a momma to run to. The rest of us would possibly have run to one too, if we'd had one. But we didn't have anybody like that.

Rufus didn't really belong there. The fact that he came from a woman like his mother, this was already very, very unusual. We just didn't have people there of highly educated backgrounds. We hadn't had any contact with this kind of thing. Rufus stood out in this regard. The boys called him "Sophocles." You might think a bunch of mountain boys wouldn't know anything about Sophocles but we all studied ancient history in those days. Rufus had that far-out dreamy nature; he was way off all the time, and that's why they started calling him Sophocles. He knew a lot of the classics, and he read beyond the age of a boy like that. It caused the students to think of him as a wise fellow, and they did it a little scornfully. The name wasn't altogether a compliment; it was a mixture of scorn and reluctant praise.

I'm sure he didn't find most of us very congenial. We were a rather crude outfit. Most of us were people who had come from places where there was a plank shack and a log cabin and an old barn and a pigpen. This was a school for poor mountain boys and most of us were just that. Some of us were poor in more ways than one. You'd meet the average fellow, and his old man was a hillbilly farmer trying to scratch a living out of two or three acres of poor farm somewhere, and not doing very

RIGHT: *Emma Agee at Stroup cottage, St. Andrew's School, c. 1920.*

CENTER: *The Stroup cottage at St. Andrew's School, where the Agees lived. (Photo courtesy Paula Tyler)*

BOTTOM: *The Agees at St. Andrew's School. (Photo courtesy Paula Tyler)*

Schoolboys at St. Andrew's School. (Photo by Father James Harold Flye)

well at it. Or worse than that: maybe a bootlegger. Many of the boys were older. One of the boys in my class was about twenty-five when he graduated, and I myself was about nineteen or twenty. I had a reputation for being a fairly rough cob. I got into an occasional fistfight. I was a hillbilly, a mountain-type. My mother had a fourth-grade education and my father had died. Rufus had a mixture of admiration and hate for me because I had paddled his tail a good many times.

I was president of the student body, and we believed in corporal punishment. Rufus was the sloppiest kid that ever lived, full of sins of omission. He never did anything that was of a vicious nature, but he couldn't get to mass on time. He'd be punished for having missed Sunday mass, or for having shown up an hour late for school, or for going over to his mother's. As I said before, that was one of the things he did—he'd run off for home. Probably the boys were beating him up or something like that and he'd take off for home. Well of course, this was a dereliction: He had failed to go to school. He'd come in front of the student council, and we would discuss the matter and vote on what the punishment would be, and if it turned out to be a paddling, it was up to me (as president of the student body) to give it to him—five or ten licks with a paddle. There was nothing brutal about it. Rufus would take it, but he didn't like it, and I'm sure he remembered it years later.

We had a strong hillbilly thing about machismo. And this boy, of course, he didn't have much of that. He suffered a great deal—probably unjustly—from people who didn't appreciate what he did have. He was no doubt a bright fellow and some of this was just pure envy or jealousy, because it was clear that he was far beyond most of us.

We used to go swimming down at the Sand Cut. It was an overgrown mudhole where they had been digging out sand. It was deep enough to swim in and quite dangerous. There was an old mowing machine sunk in one end of it, and many a boy dived in there and knocked his head on it. But we all went swimming there. The railroad came by in those days carrying passengers: the "Mountain Goat." Of course the boys went swimming naked, and when the train would come everybody had to run and jump in the water—thirty or forty naked boys of all ages and sizes. It was very amusing.

Agee and Paula Tyler at St. Andrew's School. (Photo courtesy Paula Tyler)

ABOVE: *Agee and unidentified woman at St. Andrew's School. (Photo courtesy Paula Tyler)*

RIGHT: *Agee swimming in the Sand Cut near St. Andrew's School.*

Schoolboys at St. Andrew's School.
(Photo by Father James Harold Flye)

Agee and Father Lorrie, St. Andrew's School,
c. 1920. (Photo courtesy Paula Tyler)

Father Lorrie was the monk who was directly responsible for the religious life of the boys. He was about as round as he was tall; he looked like a medieval monk, like the little round monks of the Middle Ages with their skull caps and robes. If you got in trouble, he'd call you in front of the rest of the class and say, "Hold out your hands." He had a little old cane about two feet long, and he'd just beat the devil out of your hands. But you didn't dare show any emotion; you just stood there, just like it didn't hurt one bit. And the boys just loved him. He'd come by, and these big old mountain boys would slip that little skull cap off the side of his head—just to aggravate him.

Father Flye

We used to call Jim by his middle name, Rufus. He was at that time not quite ten years old, and his sister was two years younger. I got to know them all very well. He was a very engaging boy: by nature gentle, sympathetic, affectionate, outgoing, and trusting—some fine qualities. I was awfully fond of him. We made a fine sort of friendship right away, just as soon as we got to know each other at all. He was interested in the mountain region there, the caves, the fossils in the coal seams, and natural history, and animals and their habits, and exploring South America. And we'd talk about books that he'd been reading; he read some of Booth Tarkington, I remember. He was nice and boyish and intelligent, and very, very affectionate and friendly. He had a sense of humor, but also a real sense of reverence. He was very tenderhearted and compassionate. He wouldn't for the world have done anything deliberately cruel or to cause pain, and that was very characteristic of him through his life, indeed.

Jim grew up quite familiar with the church services, and so on. He had a good verbal memory and absorbed a great deal of the words of the services, the prayer books, and the Bible, just from hearing them read. He had a good religious consciousness. There's a beautiful little passage of a few lines in the book called *Let Us Now Praise Famous Men*, a description of himself serving at an early mass. It begins: "I used as a child in the innocence of faith, to bring myself out of bed through the cold lucid water of the Cumberland morning and to serve at the altar at earliest lonely Mass, whose words were thrilling brooks of music and whose motions, a grave dance: and there between spread hands the body and blood of Christ was created among words and lifted before God in a threshing of triplicate bells." He served for me just that way many times at early mass.

Let Us Now Praise Famous Men, a curious phrase, is from the first words of a chapter in a book of the *Apocrypha* called "Ecclesiasticus." "Let us now praise famous men, and our fathers that begat us." And then it goes on to speak of past generations. He was very familiar indeed with the wording of the prayer book and Bible.

But I never thought of him as a prodigy at all. He was an intelligent child, having a good vocabulary and with quite a fund of information, as any number of children have, as a matter of fact. He was felt by any number of the boys to be in a somewhat different stratum, but that was not conscious on his part. He would rather wish to be one of the group, not to feel that "I'm of a better family" or anything like that.

I wasn't aware of his doing any writing that would be noticed until the summer that we went to Europe together, and he was to enter Phillips Exeter that fall. And the first letters from Exeter you see immediately his interest in writing, and belonging to the Lantern Club and writers that they get, and "I hope I can get some things into the magazine." But I wasn't aware in his earlier days that he had any particular gift for writing or taste for it.

James Agee

June 16, 1927

Dear Mr. Macdonald:

For the last two years I've been reading your contributions, both in the *Yale Lit* and in old numbers of the *Monthly*. A year ago last fall you wrote me—Agee is my name—an extremely nice letter saying about the same sort of things I want to say. After reading as much as I have of your writing, I feel I can say it with more reason.

It is this: that we evidently write and think remarkably alike. That

RIGHT: *Agee at Exeter. Yearbook photo, 1928.*

BELOW: *The Lantern Club, Exeter Yearbook. Agee on right, front row. Date unknown.*

at least to certain known extents our likes and dislikes are the same—and that we had a good deal the same difficulties with the *Monthly*. One interest I know positively we have in common—interest in moving pictures, especially from the director's point of view. For next year, as president of the Lantern Club, I'm doing my best to get *Variety*, *Potemkin* and such films up here. This year we had *The Last Laugh* with about as much popular success as elsewhere. At any rate, I was able to convince a few members of the faculty of the possibilities of the movies.

I'm wandering from what I want to say, though—I'm not sure whether or not these common interests and similarities in style would palm out successfully into a correspondence acquaintanceship, but I'm most anxious to try it. Simply discussing movies, or each other's stories—or whatever you like.

Last September I first read your story "Wall"—about the rise and decline of a friendship, if you don't happen to remember. It interested me then, and I liked it immensely. During this last term almost precisely the same thing has happened to me—I being the Morris Cotesworth—the one who suffers. In my case there were consequences which you may possibly have thought of, but did not suggest—I was almost drowned in psychological meanderings too dreary and far too long for any story. Quite frequently I've been on the verge of suicide. Possibly mine was a more serious case, all the way through, though. At any rate, "Wall" is now more to me than Gospel. I read it over and recognize symptoms in every sentence. Were you yourself ever in such a fix? It seems impossible that you could have imagined so minutely such a story.

Incidentally, what a hell of a tragedy friendship can become, can't it? Worst of all, apparently all but thickhead friendships must run that very course.

Did you by chance work in Ohio last summer? "At Threshing Time" gave me that feeling. The dialect was interestingly like that of a Tennessee mountaineer.

I suppose this has all the unpleasant earmarks of a "pickup." I apologize, but again beg you to write.

Very sincerely,
J. R. Agee

Dear Dwight [Macdonald]:

32

I'm damned if I know what I'm going to write, for, contrary to what you say, I'm almost continuously at a loss for something to say. Of course I might try to be funny about my rotten typing, if I weren't sure that next to Back-Seat Driving, that is the most hackneyed dope in existence for humorous comment.

I'd be grateful for a hoe and convenient corn; I'm finding life intolerably boring this summer. During the winter my Dream Super-Cutie went to a "woman's" college, where she achieved several additional and superfluous pounds of hip, democratic tastes in necking and a dim-witted brand of sophistication which is more nauseating than baffling, as she fervently hopes it is. With her out of the way, there's nothing more diverting than an occasional movie and some glorious scenery. Few things can beat a misty sunrise. . . .

I always look forward to my summers as time for writing without interruption. They're worse than school! I haven't the courage to drive away my friends, so I get practically nothing done. During all last summer and so far now, I've written only about 20,000 words on the would-be novel. Worst of all, I feel that my howl about lack of time is mainly bluff; this morning I have time—I took it, and could do nothing with it. . . .

To me the great thing about the movies is that it's a brand-new field. I don't see how much more can be done with writing or with the stage. In fact, every kind of recognized "art" has been worked pretty nearly to the limit. Of course great things will undoubtedly be done in all of them, but, possibly excepting music, I don't see how they can avoid being at least in part imitations. As for the movies, however, their possibilities are infinite—that is, insofar as the possibilities of an art CAN be so. So far as I can see, all that's been done so far is to show that art is really possible on the screen. We've barely begun to stir the fringes of their possibilities, though. Some guy in the *Theatre Arts Monthly* says that, because of the limitations set on the personality of the actors, through the loss of voice and actual presence, and because of the like failure to set up actual scenery before the audience, realism is impossible

The Swim Team, Exeter Yearbook. Agee in last row on left. Date unknown.

in the movies. Rot! Did you see *Stark Love*, or *Greed?* Then you know the ridiculousness of that! Can writing or drama hope to rub your nose in realism as the movies do? Could *Potemkin* have been staged or described to even approximate the realism of the movie itself? I don't see how. . . .

Robert Saudek

He was not what one would call a typical college student, by any means. The first thing I was aware of was an enormous energy. He walked with tremendous vigor, and kind of whistled in an excited way and thrust his head about, and so on.

And another immediate impression was that there was a certain mystery about him that I think everyone who ever met him felt. Some people would find it amusing. There was a quality about him that was unpredictable. He would say he was going out somewhere for, maybe a walk along the Charles River, on a winter night, and he would go out and disappear for two days. And no one ever asked him where he had been. He was never a person to infringe on anyone else's privacy, and everyone was extremely sensitive of his privacy.

I was from the Midwest and was really quite young and inexperienced. Jim, while he was from an even more rural community than I, having come from the South, nevertheless had come north to go to Exeter for preparation for college. Consequently, he seemed quite a mature person to me.

He was not hard to come to know, extremely warm and accessible in conversation, and extraordinarily interested in anything anybody had to say. He seemed to have a great sense of interest in what people had on their minds, which was very flattering to someone who's just arrived at that big university.

I think Jim had a sense of great pride in himself, a sense of self-confidence which belied his ordinary manner, his ordinary sensitivity. He had quite a number of circles of friends. A great many people wanted to be his friend. He was rather demanding of friends. He liked interesting people, and he liked people who were prepared to sit up and talk all night, or go off—he was such an impulsive person—just go off and do something. I tried to keep up with him, but not with any great success. Certainly he had faculty friends, which I always thought was very interesting. He got to know Ted Spencer, who was a prominent young man on the English faculty, and he got to know Ivor Richards very well. I think faculty people, younger teachers, realized that they had a genius on their hands. Anyone who recognizes that in a person is delighted to know him better and care about him and see a lot of him. Indeed, he was rare enough as an individual, as a human being, that people did feel they were in touch with somebody who was a "one of a kind" person.

He was well known as a poet. He was president of the *Advocate*, which in his period was a very distinguished literary magazine in college circles. His name was well known as a poet among people who would care about things like that, and he devoted a great deal of time to writing. He liked to write at night, and he tended to write in enormous spurts of enthusiasm and energy. He would go all night long and end up with that tiny little squiggle that he wrote on yellow paper, all uphill. And by morning he would end up with stories or poems, which he would generally read to me or to somebody.

James Agee

April 24, 1929

Dear Macdonald—

A fellow in my dormitory owns a movie camera and has done some interesting work with it. He's worked out a good deal, unassisted, about lighting and has a few test shots for a movie he was thinking of making last summer. At present, it's possible we'll make two movies; one a sort of *$24 Island* of Boston. There's no chance for such beautiful stuff as Flaherty got in that, but Boston has a real individuality that may be fun to try to photograph. The idea is that I'll devise shots, angles, camera work, etc.—and stories; he'll take care of the photography and lighting. The other thing is a story I wrote last fall. I've worked a good bit of it into pictures already. . . . The difficulty is finding good actors. It wouldn't be very expensive: we intend to make it in three reels; it would be necessary to hire two tenement rooms for a while. Here's one thing I particularly like:

The man has found his wife in a faint on the floor. He carries her into the dark bedroom: a quick close-up shows his hand groping for the light; he turns it on and it begins a violent swinging. He puts her on the bed and stands above her for a moment. The audience has reason to know that a discovery is imminent which will mean hell for the wife. The camera now peers around his back, and discovers her lying beneath the swinging, bending shadow thrown by the moving light.

I doubt we'll ever do anything with it, but we're in for a good deal of fun, I think.

I'm trying to write a paper on the possibilities of the talkies—which I despise. Nevertheless, great things (not in the movie manner) could be done with them. Both depend on the possibility of fusing pictures, sound, and in one case color, into a unity. One is—that they could be a fulfillment of all that Blake wanted to do—great pictures, poetry, color and music—the other is the chance they offer Joyce and his followers. I should think they'd go wild over the possibilities of it. I wrote a story last spring which I'd give anything to make as a "test case"—but I somehow feel a traitor to the movies as they should be, even to think of such things.

November 19, 1930

Dear Father Flye.

So far as I can tell, I definitely want to write. Nothing else holds me in the same way. I had two other interests just as strong a few years ago—music and directing movies. Last spring I was all but ready to quit college and bum to California and trust to luck for the rest. But from now on I'm committed to writing with a horrible definiteness. In fact, it amounts to a rather unhealthy obsession. I'm thinking about it every waking minute in one way or another, and my head is spinning and often dull with the continuous overwork. It sounds conceited, but I'd do anything on earth to become a really great writer. That's as sincere a thing as I've ever said. Do you see though where it leads me?

LEFT: *Yearbook picture, 1932.*

BELOW: *The* Advocate *Board, Harvard Yearbook, 1932.*

Robert Saudek

At the end of the first year in college, Jim wanted to go west. He was very interested in, well, what then would have been called "the common man." That was in the Depression; the Crash had come nearly a year

before, and he was anxious to go out and meet people and listen to them and talk to them and know them. He wanted to *try* to be one of them. It was interesting that he really wanted to try to be like those people, and experience what they experienced. He had a certain reverence for poverty and simplicity. So he did go out, he did hitchhike. He went to the wheat fields—starting in the South and moving north with the crop—I guess it was almost a gypsy life; the people changed as he moved. It was a preview, in a sense, of the period when he went south in preparation for writing *Let Us Now Praise Famous Men*.

James Agee

May 10, 1929

Dear Dwight [Macdonald],

I'm going to spend the summer working in the wheat fields, starting in Oklahoma in June. The thing looks good in every way. I've never worked, and greatly prefer such a job; I like to get drunk and will; I like to sing and learn both dirty songs and hobo ones and will; and I like the heterogeneous gang that moves north on the job. You get a wonderful mess of bums and lumberjacks, so I'm told. Also I like bumming, and shall do as much of it as I can. Finally, I like saving money and this promises from five to seven a day. It will be hellishly hard work, so for once I won't have a chance to worry and feel like hell all summer. I'm afraid it sounds a little as if I were a lousy Bohemian and lover of the Earthy Earthy, but I assure I'm nothing so foul, quite, as that. . . .

Agee at Harvard, 1932. (Photo courtesy Olivia Wood)

Maybe August 1 [1929]
Oshkosh, Nebraska
c/o Mr. John Hutchinson

Dear Dwight [Macdonald]:

If pen and ink and white paper gave you trouble, this should rival the Rosetta Stone. To add insult to injury, it's written in a wagon-bed— about my only chance to write is between loads.

Am now working at hauling and scooping grain on a "combine" crew. With that I was on the go every minute and loading on rough ground wasn't exactly fun. I rammed a pitchfork into my Achilles tendon and it gave me a good deal of trouble when I went on the road again.

Kansas is the most utterly lousy state I've ever seen. Hot as hell and trees ten miles apart. I worked near a town which proudly bore the name "Glade" because of a clump of scrawny, dusty little trees it had somehow managed to assemble.

The first town across the Nebraska line was so different I declared a holiday, sat on a bench in the courthouse park, and wrote a story. I rather think I've stumbled onto the best possible surroundings, and state of mind, in which to write. I certainly was more at home with it than at Harvard, home, or Exeter. . . .

Have you ever done any bumming? It's a funny business. In 24 hours I made over six hundred miles; in 23 I failed to make 28, was caught simultaneously by night and a cloudburst. I hope the good sort of luck prevails when I try to get home. I'm going to try to make it in 5 or 6 days, on ten dollars.

Have to tackle a load now,

Jim

December 1929

Dear Dwight [Macdonald],

. . . I neglected to write Mother for several weeks and letters boomeranged from various Kansas P.O.'s long before I returned home. They were quite sure I'd died several deaths, and had worked more adventures than I could have imagined in a year. Within two days of

Rockland I had my only really personal acquaintance with danger: a boy picked me up in the Pennsylvania mountains at 2 A.M. and drove off a mountain curve at 45 m.p.h. The car turned over three times, but the only injury sustained was a cut on my wrist and the startling bouleversement of a roast beef sandwich I'd just eaten. . . .

Father Flye

His first wife, Olivia Saunders, was the daughter of Dr. Saunders, who was a professor of chemistry at Hamilton College near Clinton, New York. They were a highly cultivated family. One time Dr. Saunders wanted to get an assistant in the chemistry department, and he stipulated that the man must be a competent chemist, of course, but he must by all means be a good cello player. Dr. Saunders would get a little group together and play chamber music half the night and that kind of thing. Jim met Olivia Saunders at Radcliffe when she was a student there, and he, at Harvard.

Olivia Saunders Wood

The time when we first met—it was Ivor Richards who was in the middle of all that really. I was in Cambridge taking classes, studying with Ivor among other people, and we all went up to my parents' house in Clinton. Jim came, too; I met him then. That was in 1931. It's a fairly big house, and everybody was very friendly and excited about things, a very stimulating atmosphere. We may have read plays; we used to do that a lot in the house. We would take parts and read a Shakespeare play. And Ivor read aloud a lot; he was a wonderful talker and a wonderful reader. I remember Ivor reading things like *Ash Wednesday* in an unforgettable way. The Spencers would have been there, Nancy and Ted. Ted Spencer was teaching English at Harvard then, and Jim knew Ted very well. I think Ted was very interested in him. Jim sort of charmed everybody. He was a very exciting person. He was the kind of guy who fitted in with any age, you know, because we were somewhat older.

Clockwise from left: *Ted Spencer with baby, Arthur Percy Saunders, Nancy Spencer, James Agee, and Louise Saunders in front of the Saunders home in Clinton, New York, 1932. (Photo courtesy Olivia Wood)*

Clockwise from left: *Nancy Spencer, Louise Saunders, James Agee, and Ted Spencer with baby in front of the Saunders home in Clinton, New York, 1932. (Photo courtesy Olivia Wood)*

Top speed—yes, I felt that—I think we all did. A kind of intensified emotional thing. Later on, when I was in Cambridge taking classes, we saw an awful lot of him and some of his friends. They would come over and have meals and sit up talking and have a wonderful time. I wouldn't have any idea what we talked about. I suppose we talked about literature and ideas and ourselves and movies and psychoanalysis. Jim was very interested in psychoanalysis. He thought he'd like to be an analyst at one point.

Robert Fitzgerald

Certainly the most exciting of all Jim's instructors at Harvard was Ivor Richards. In my sophomore year, when Jim was a junior, Richards came. He'd been to China, and on his way back to Cambridge in England, so to speak, he stopped off at Harvard. He was there for one term, doing a course in the history of modern English literature, and a course that he had invented at Cambridge called "Practical Criticism." Now here was an extremely well trained, very lucid mind, trained in psychology at Cambridge, therefore with a certain scientific background, applying itself with passion to modern English literature. You know, there are professors, and there are professors, and what was especially true of Richards was that one felt with him that he was a participant in the work of literature. He was working on the edge of literature himself, as a psychologist and as a mind, to *make something*, in the same way that a born writer like Jim Agee was also. There was a feeling of kinship, and that makes all the difference.

From these lectures and these classes James Agee got, I think, a certain edge of literary perception that he wouldn't possibly have gained anywhere else—a kind of sharpness of mind applied to writing. For a time it enabled him to hold in a kind of equilibrium the American experience of which he was very conscious as a boy from Knoxville, who had the Cumberland Plateau in his blood so to speak, and the experience of an eastern prep school. These two things, the Anglo-American or English heritage and the specifically American one of Tennessee, were two sides of his nature that he was able, for a couple of years at least and partly due to Richards's influence, to hold in equilibrium and to make something of. His poems done during those two years had a greater degree, to my mind, of solidity as works of art—the effect of integrating these two parts of his nature.

Dwight Macdonald

He graduated from Harvard in 1932. That was the depth of the Depression, and as you know, he was a man of no money, like myself, poor boy. I had happened to get a job on *Fortune* in '29, and Agee, with whom I'd been in correspondence since '27, told me he needed a job, and I talked to Ralph Ingersoll, the editor of *Fortune*, and Ingersoll was very receptive to the idea and said, "Yes; I know about Agee." Then it turned out that it was really Luce who knew about Agee, because Agee had done a parody issue of *Time* for the Harvard *Advocate*, and Luce had been very impressed by it. So I guess they gave him the usual tests, but Agee could write anything with his left hand, and so he was hired. And he was there for much too long of course.

James Agee

May 1932

Dear Dwight [Macdonald]—

Back tonight, found your letter and noted contents with eyes rolling upward and stomach downward for joy, relief, gratitude and such things. I shall send a wire in the morning to beat this letter down.

The thing chiefly on my mind is, I don't want to ruin any chances of losing this chance (for which I thank you, God, and Managing Editor Ingersoll). Taking your letter perfectly literally, there seems to be no need of coming down before graduation. But: should I? If it makes absolutely no difference, I shan't; my money is low and my time crammed, one way and another. But if it makes—if there's any doubt about my qualifying and what not—*any* reason why it would be well for me to come down—will you please let me know?

My chief business has been reading, writing, and (thanks to a generous and evil-intentioned friend) Solitary Drinking. The writing has been mostly (a) a good start on a rather chaotic, messy play about two decaying girls and assorted boyfriends, (b) a bad start on what should be a great play if I were a great playwright (I stole the plot from Marston and in trying to account for Elizabethan extravagances in 1930 life the whole thing has gone too Dostoyevsky for the stage and (c) about 250 lines of a new somewhat cockeyed narrative poem. The poetry is, on the whole, a flop, but I'm fool enough to have faith in the idea; vaguely—that I can take a somewhat stock bawdy situation, fit it to characters common to Chaucer and to midwestern "realistic" novels— and make something of it Chaucer at best wouldn't vomit on. Only it would seem to take practice, very careful study, and about ten times the talent and five times the guts I have, to do it. The Solitary Drinking has proceeded, quietly but firmly, throughout; modest, but effective—alcohol, water, juniper juice and lemon. Palatable in hot weather, God forbid. . . .

Words fail me re the job: besides the fairly fundamental fact that I don't want to starve. There are dozens of reasons I want a job and many more why I am delighted to get this one.

Very sincerely,
Jim

August 1932

Dear Father Flye,

When you get down here again I'll have my phonograph working in my office to play at night. An empty skyscraper is just about an ideal place for it. Something attracts me very much about playing Beethoven's Ninth Symphony there, with all New York about 600 feet below you and with that swell ode taking in the whole earth, and with everyone on earth supposedly singing it, and all except joy forgotten.

Agee, c. 1933. (Courtesy Mia Agee)

August 1932

Dear Olivia [Saunders Wood],

In some cases I am not sure of the value of never fooling yourself, and writing is one of the cases. I think as a rule you are as small a writer as you feel, and if by any combination of fool circumstances you manage to feel like a great one, you have then at worst a fighting chance you'd otherwise lack.

Olivia Saunders Wood

We got married in January of 1933, and we got this nice apartment on Perry Street and started living there, and that was very, very nice. It was a two-room basement apartment, with a yard, and in the spring we'd put pansies in it. And we used the porch and lived outdoors a great deal. It was the kind of thing that was just nice when you didn't have much money. You didn't need any more room than that. Jim was just starting in with *Fortune*.

Robert Fitzgerald

He and Via had really a rather nice apartment on Perry Street, one of those old streets in the Village, a rather quiet street then. It was comfortable and well furnished, a very decent place to live. I, of course, was there every once in a while for dinner and for an evening, and the routine was pleasant and not too unusual. He was then working at *Fortune*, and he had gotten a certain command of how to do that. He knew how to do the *Fortune* thing and was doing it successfully. I think he had had a raise; they had entrusted to him a big story on the TVA, and he was doing well. They had a piano, of course. Jim loved to play the piano and played it by the hour. And they also kept a sailboat at City Island—a sloop, or maybe just a catboat. On Sundays they would take the subway out to City Island and sail and swim. So he and Via were living there, fairly contentedly and fairly productively during that time, say '33, '34, '35. The expedition to Alabama, which gave rise to the tenant farmer book, of course, brought all that to an end.

Dwight Macdonald

As I say, he could write about anything, but he couldn't write about business, and that was one trouble because *Fortune* was supposed to be a business magazine. He'd write articles on the ten most precious jewels of the world, private islands, luxury cruises, furs (and you can imagine what he'd do with that). He'd bring a tremendous cultural weight to it, and also he would write with this extremely brilliant and marvelous incantatory style—rich, beautiful prose.

And then one day Luce noticed that he had written no business articles. Well, we all tried to get out of writing business articles, but I, being a more normal hack, would do it. So he assigned Agee an article on the price of steel rails. And his point was that they had not changed in price since 1892, not even by one penny, and this was an example of monopoly pricing obviously. And he edited it himself. He said, "I'm going to make Agee into a business writer." But Agee couldn't understand why this was of any interest, and Luce would say, "Jim, don't you understand that since 1892 there hasn't been a change in the price of steel rails?" And Agee would say, "Well, yes, but so," expecting something more. Well, there wasn't any more.

James Agee

October 1933

Dear Father Flye,

The editor-in-chief was much impressed by my Tennessee Valley story—one of the best pieces of writing he'd ever seen in *Fortune*. He was as honest and swell as anyone could wish for, but what it will profit me to become a good economist, I don't see. If I had as much confidence about writing as I have intention, everything might be much easier. I feel the well-known prison walls distinctly thickening.

Olivia Saunders Wood

We had a very good life there, but as I look back on it, it was extremely populated, because Jim was so stimulating that he was surrounded by people all the time, friends who always wanted to come see him. And preferably they would sit up very late at night. We all would. Jim was on that rhythm of a person who doesn't want to get up in the morning and wakes up about twelve, has breakfast, and then goes up to the office and comes back very late in the afternoon. And then if we had company or felt like it, he'd get to talking in the evening, and get more and more bright and stimulating as the evening went on. You know that rhythm; people are very different in their rhythms. I'm a morning person, but I remember that's what he did.

49

Dwight Macdonald

He talked in a rather low tone—he never raised his voice—rather monotonous in a way, and he used to give emphasis by using his hands all the time. He was always shaping things. He couldn't talk without his hands at all. I would say he was interesting because in one sense he was a monologist; he would get going on something. But in another way though, if you insisted on interrupting him, he would be able to deal with your arguments. He wasn't just a rhapsodizer. He was an interesting combination of someone like Thomas Wolfe, who didn't have much brains really; he was simply a gusher. And Agee was that, too, but Agee also had the T. S. Eliot, or the hard, critical, intellectual side to him, too. So he could do both.

Robert Fitzgerald

His talking was very physical. The hands came in very much. He had in his mind a sense of form, and the form that he wanted to give to his discourse he was also, so to speak, putting in the air with his hands, his fingers, and so on. One felt that what he was saying was reinforced by his whole body; he was talking with it, and in particular his hands and arms.

So, when you were talking with Jim and the conversation was serious, you were involved in what, I suppose, from an objective point of view, from someone who was looking through a window, would have seemed a performance really. And he did also have histrionic ability. He was wonderful at parodying certain kinds of voice, a Tennessee hillbilly voice, for example, applied to the recitation of a poem by Shelley. Imagine.

Dwight Macdonald

But the worst thing was, once he got seated in a place, whether his own or some other guy's, my God, it would be three or four o'clock and Agee was still there with a few devoted souls, and there was no chance of their ever leaving.

He never gave up; he would simply stay up all night. Or would spend twenty minutes arguing a minor point. There was something obsessive about it, which is a sign of a certain kind of genius, too.

He couldn't define himself. That was his great trouble as a writer, too. He couldn't limit himself; he was oceanic. And in a way that was his great strength, too.

Robert Fitzgerald

There was no moderation ever possible, you know. The man was immoderate in every way. His interests were immoderately wide, his intellect was immoderately intense, and his passions were immoderately large. This was true at Harvard and became even truer in New York and later.

He was a revolutionary, in a sense, on too many fronts. He was a revolutionary against revolutionaries, among other things, and it wasn't merely capitalists with whom he found fault, but also their opponents. It became, as I sometimes thought, almost tedious to hear Jim examining all sides of any given question, all sides turned out to be unsatisfactory in the end; and they did, of course. He was right. So this made it impossible for him, for example, to join the Communist party or do anything like that. He saw what was wrong there just as clearly as he saw what was wrong with capitalism. Everybody could see what was wrong with capitalism; they had made a great mess of it. But he also perceived what was wrong with Stalinist communism, in which he was proved

Agee, 1937. (Photo by Walker Evans. Courtesy of the estate of Walker Evans)

abundantly right later in the decade. Here was a complicated mind and a complicated man facing and trying to make sense of the phenomena of the 1930s in this country, and that in itself was very exciting to watch, because nothing cheap and nothing easy was ever acceptable to him. That's all there was to it.

Dwight Macdonald

Meeting Agee, anybody could see that here was a rather original, extraordinary person. I would say it would be hard to know Agee at all well, if you have any sensitivity to literary stuff, without realizing that here was a somebody who was extremely expressive. And then when you saw anything he wrote—well, I would say that he was the most brilliant, the deepest, most creative prose writer of my generation. And I think most people realized that.

But of course a number of people were repelled by him. As Dr. Johnson once said, "I have no passion for clean linen," and this was true of Agee, too. I mean, he didn't change his shirt as much as he might have. As Walker Evans says in that marvelous four-page introduction to the new edition of *Let Us Now Praise Famous Men*, "His tailors were wind, rain, fog, and dishevelment," or something. In fact, his suits were molded to his body after a while. He never had his suits pressed or anything like that. Also, he had rather bad teeth, which he never bothered to do anything about either. Some people didn't like that.

Not that he was aggressive, even when he was drunk, and he was drunk quite a lot. He was a nice drunk, as far as I ever knew him anyway. He was obviously somebody very strange. And hearing him talk, hearing this incantation that he would make with words, you would realize that here was somebody who had extraordinary verbal power.

Olivia Saunders Wood

I thought of him as a person who suffered an awful lot. He had a great deal of unhappiness in his work; I think that his sort of genius saw that a thing might have been so much better than what he actually got down in words—it bothered him a terrible lot. He used to get frightfully depressed and say "I can't write; I can't work," and of course part of the problem was that he was taking out a lot of creative energy in those *Fortune* years, and then trying to work in the evenings. He'd bang his head on the wall and say "I'm no good" and that sort of thing. He talked a little about suicide, enough so that I thought, well, he won't ever do that.

I learned how to make scenes from Jim, because I was brought up not to cry and not to get angry and all that. So I thought if Jim's going to do it, I'll do it, too. So we'd have scenes and we'd both feel a great deal better. But just a very lively, extraordinary temperament to live with, and some of it showed torture really. It's a very private kind of suffering, that kind of suffering.

And then wonderful vitality and highs at other times. He had an enormous ability to enjoy life, too—and all those talents, and the wonderful sense of humor. The guy was so humorous, terrific. I adored him. I was crazy about him.

James Agee

1934

Dear Father Flye:

I'm in most possible kinds of pain, mental and spiritual. The trouble revolves chiefly around the simple-sounding problem of how to become what I wish I could, when I can't. That, however, is fierce and complicated enough to keep me balancing over suicide as you might lean out over the edge of a high building. My ideas and impressions and desires, which are much larger than I can begin to get to paper, are loose in my brains like wild beasts, not devouring each other, but in the process of tearing the zoo apart.

Robert Fitzgerald

When I got to New York and got to working on the newspaper there, we would often get together to compare notes on life and the world. We

Agee, 1937. (Photo by Walker Evans. Courtesy of the estate of Walker Evans)

would, of course, think and talk about other possibilities beyond jour-nalism, and one of them was that of being a forest ranger. I think he was attracted by that kind of thing. And if he had done that, the results might have been very interesting. That is, if he had given himself that kind of isolation and that kind of time he might have done a great deal more writing, of his own I mean, during the years when he was grinding it out for Luce.

Another thing that I remember we became very interested in was the news that the government was selling a lot of old lighthouses, no longer needed along the coast, and wouldn't it be great, you know, if we could muster enough money to buy a lighthouse and move there, to get away from the world and New York in particular. Well, of course, we never did.

Olivia Saunders Wood

He loved to talk and communicate and have people communicate with him. He loved that, and he was wonderful at it, and this takes a lot of time. I used to think, Oh dear, this is eating up his time, but after all it was something he needed just as much, this direct human contact, rather than shutting himself up with a piece of paper and writing. He knew that he was destined to be a creative writer, and that was that. He couldn't kid himself about it. He wanted to be a great writer, there's no question of it. I think that writing was like a master in his life. Writing was what he was serving; that's what you felt. He couldn't get away from it. I think there was a lot of trying to escape, like the drinking and probably all the people and the talk. But he needed all that; that was natural to him. It was a very strong, constant thing in his life that he was going to write and write well. *The* thing. It was never away from his mind much, I don't think. This fact of needing to write and wanting to write, and wanting it to be just as good as it possibly could be. He had very high standards that way really. When I was married to him, I thought nothing should interfere with this, if possible. Not interrupt it and not take his mind off it when it was going well, keep distractions out. You know, a wife doing that kind of thing. You can see it—keep it quiet for him.

Robert Fitzgerald

Oh, it was unforgettable! He came to my office door. "Robert, have you got a moment?" Swallowing hard. He must just have come down from upstairs where he had been given this assignment, and he was terribly excited. He told me that not only were they going to send him to Alabama on this assignment, but that they were going to allow him to have Walker Evans, which was, I guess, a degree of generosity and taste on their part that he hadn't expected. Anyway, the prospect of going to Alabama with Evans, whose work he so much admired, tremendously excited him, and nothing would do but we had to knock off work at once and go over to a bar on Third Avenue to have some beers and talk it over.

Well, I think he knew in his bones that this was going to be something big for him, you know. He knew, that given a month or two months in the Deep South, looking into the lives of the impoverished was going to electrify a great deal of his nature that had not yet been given an opportunity for full expression or for full employment, that this was going to test him and all that he had much more than anything that had ever come up before. So he was scared. Scared clean through of facing this thing. All the moral, physical, intellectual questions that this would bring up with a man as sensitive and as complicated as Jim Agee were suddenly activated, do you see, and he knew that afternoon that it was going to be a great thing for him.

James Agee

June 18, 1936

Dear Father Flye,

I must cut this short and do a week's work in the next twenty hours or so. I've been assigned to do a story on a "sharecropper family—daily and yearly life" and also a study of farm economics in the South. The best break I ever had on *Fortune*; feel terrific personal responsibility toward story, considerable doubts of my ability to bring it off, considerable more doubts of *Fortune*'s ultimate willingness to use it. Will be starting South Saturday, for a month's work.

Dwight Macdonald

There was one movie I remember, we both discovered sort of independently and communicated with each other about it, by—that was 1928—by Karl Brown, called *Stark Love*. It was a semi-documentary fictional movie about the hillbillies in the Appalachians. The title is a cheap title, but the movie is a really extraordinary film. Very, very severe, very Walker Evans in a way. Karl Brown became a minor director—he never did very much else. But this was a thing that was in that realistic vein that Agee had a special feeling for; it cut through all the clichés. It was completely unromantic, and very severe, very austere. And this must have been in his mind when he went down to somewhat the same area—a little bit farther south—to write, to look at these sharecroppers' families. I'm sure he was thinking of that movie.

FROM Let Us Now Praise Famous Men

During July and August 1936 Walker Evans and I were traveling in the middle south of this nation, and were engaged in what, even from the first, has seemed to me rather a curious piece of work. It was our business to prepare, for a New York magazine, an article on cotton tenantry in the United States, in the form of a photographic and verbal record of the daily living and environment of an average white family of tenant farmers. We had first to find and live with such a family; and that was the object of our traveling. . . . More essentially, this is an independent inquiry into certain normal predicaments of human divinity. . . . If complications arise, that is because {we} are trying to deal with it not as journalists, sociologists, politicians, entertainers, humanitarians, priests, or artists, but seriously. . . .

Down in front of the courthouse Walker had picked up talk with you, Fred Ricketts . . . and then two men came up and stood shyly, a little away; they were you, George {Gudger}, and you, {Bud Woods}. . . .

{W}e drove you out home . . . and there on the side porch of the house Walker made pictures, with the big camera; and we sat around and talked, eating the small sweet peaches . . . and drinking the warm and fever-tasting

water from the cistern sunk beneath the porch; and we kept you from your dinners an hour at least. . . .

{T}here you all are, the mother as before a firing squad, the children like columns of an exquisite temple, their eyes straying, and behind, both girls, bent deep in the dark shadow somehow as if listening and as in a dance, attending like harps the black flags of their hair . . . I can remember it so clearly, as if it were five minutes ago . . . when the whole time was like one chord and shock of music.

Walker Evans

The people we lived with were hard to find. We needed a practically suitable subject that would give us entrée. You couldn't just go up to somebody's house and say "I want to come in here and live here." That had to be created by tact, and not everybody was malleable to that. But we did find some people who understood us, and we told them exactly what we were doing, and they said all right. I think it was really largely because they liked Agee, who had a great gift of making people not only like him, but love him. They only had to listen to him a little bit, and they took him in. I just sort of followed his lead that way. Although I did pick up the family first, he took on from there.

Elizabeth Tingle

Now as far as how they found us, I couldn't say. The first thing we knew they came up and introduced themselves, and told us where they were from. And then they got to taking pictures, Walker did, and he was writing down little things, you know.

At the start it was a little hard for us to understand them, but I'll tell you, there wasn't any harm said to one, or anybody made fun of them or anything. You could understand them, but they just sounded funny. I asked Mr. Jimmy, I said, "What kind of sound does your voice got?" He said, "That is the northern kind of talk. All of them up there's

Frank Tingle, Bud Fields, and Floyd Burroughs, Greensboro,
Alabama, 1936. (Photo by Walker Evans)

Tingle children, Floyd Burroughs at left, 1936.
(Photo by Walker Evans)

Elizabeth Tingle. (Photo by Walker Evans)

like that." But you know when they left here, they had got to where they was talking our kind of talk.

Ellie Mae Burroughs

The big people, you know, the big bugs around Moundville, they would tell us that they was spies from Russia, and that they was trying to get all they could out of the United States. I don't know what spies does, dear, but anyway we knowed that they wasn't going to hurt us, and they didn't.

I don't know why they'd say such things about them. They just didn't know them was all. I reckon they was more or less afraid of them because they thought that they was in here for some harm. I don't know what made them feel that way. Afraid they might tell us some way to get by, tell us some way to make a better living, so we wouldn't have to dig it out with them, you see. It was the landlords mostly.

It was in the time of the war and they was afraid to take them into their homes to keep them or have anything to do with them. They was afraid they'd come over here, you know, and see what was going on in our country and then they'd go back and they'd know more how to come over and harm us some way or another. But after I talked with them awhile, well, I didn't see nothing to be afraid of. I knowed that they couldn't hurt me 'cause we was having a hard enough time anyway. If they just didn't kill us, that's all.

They stayed there with us; they eat with us and everything. I fixed their breakfast every morning, and their supper every night. We'd have a lot of fun around the table, you know. They was just like us; they was just common people. 'Course I knowed they had plenty. But they was good mixers. He'd stay around the house with me and see what I done. Like I churned to make the butter; they couldn't understand how I done that. And he'd stay around there and watch me put up the milk, and what I'd do every morning when I'd first get up, and follow me all day. And then it come back in the book what he had done. I don't care what they done with their books and things; if they got rich off it, it was all right with me. It was the truth. Tell you the truth about it, when they

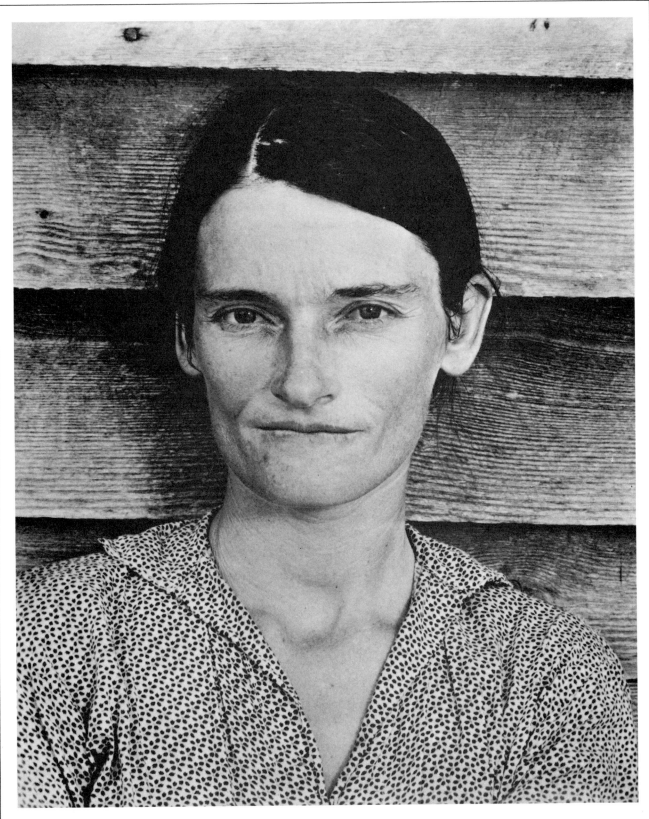

Ellie Mae Burroughs. (Photo by Walker Evans)

left here, I hated to see them go. I could have cried if it'd done any good, 'cause I had got attached to 'em.

One day I remember he got up and asked me what I was gonna do that day. See, we was on the farm and it took us all in the field, and what time we wasn't in the field we was doing other things. He told me if I got through that day, he wanted to talk with me a little bit, if I had time, and I told him I would. So we sat down to the table when I got a little caught up, and he started asking me what I did in the morning when I first got up, and I told him all the little jobs that I done at home, and then I'd go to the fields, you know. Well, he couldn't see how I had time to do what I done at the house and then go to the field, see. But I had to, see. And he wondered how I could do all that. We had to go. That was all there was to it. They was cotton and corn, you know, and it takes a lot of work for cotton. They was there with us part of the time when we was making the crop and then they stayed with us 'til over in gatherin' time. It was just hard work. We made our own syrup; we put the whole family to work.

My oldest daughter, she was big enough that she'd go with them anywhere they went, and she loved both of them. They'd get up and let her get dressed, what she had to dress with, you know, and they'd take her with them all through the country. She knowed where places was and all. And people even got to tellin' me that they might harm her some way. Well I wasn't afraid to let her go with them and all, 'cause I knew they wasn't going to hurt her.

Walker Evans

We were friends, and we were both working rather defiantly really. Agee and I worked in distant harmony, paying no attention really, by agreement, to each other, but working on the same subject. Our styles were admittedly very different, but we had enormous respect for each other and a great interest and intensity about that work. We were quite young. Agee, I think, was only twenty-seven years old. I must have been about thirty-three or thirty-four.

I was absorbed in the technical and aesthetic task to such an extent

Floura Lee Tingle with Walker Evans's shadow.
(Photo by Walker Evans)

that what my reaction was was really one of professional pleasure: I knew I had some very rich material to work with and I was excited to work with it. I didn't identify myself subjectively nearly as much as Agee did. I was working objectively on the visual material in front of me, which was incredibly rich. That was really hard work, but not thought of as such at the time. If you're young and interested, as we were, you throw yourself into work like that without any thought of sparing yourself, or without any thought of the time invested or energy either. That is work at its best, the way all work ought to be, and seldom is.

Elizabeth Tingle

I can just see them in my mind. One of them taking pictures and the other one writing down things. We didn't understand what he was doing; he was just writing down things. I just thought it was his business, and it wasn't nothing for me to wonder about. He was going to put them in a magazine. He'd ask Mama and them questions about how they was working, and he saw how we had to live. He asked them how much they got for a crop, you know, and Papa told them that we just couldn't make it hardly, said we'd hardly have enough to get Christmas. They'd have to get Christmas stuff on the credit starting the next year.

We was making anywhere from ten to fifteen to twenty bales of cotton on a year, and we wasn't getting but fifteen dollars a month to live on. Yes sir, we lived on fifteen dollars a month while we was working in the field. Now Papa made more than that when he was working in the pine woods, but him and Mama said they didn't see how we got by. There was six of us children and Mama and Papa—and fifteen dollars a month. Well, I do see how we got by. Because we raised our corn, raised our cornbread, and we raised our meat and lard, and they just had to buy stuff they couldn't raise. You take feeding eight, on fifteen dollars a month.

Ellie Mae Burroughs

The Tidmores owned the most of the land. You couldn't hardly get a place with nobody else 'cause they owned it all, and they just took everything people made. They were supposed to furnish us groceries all the year to make this crop on. Well, if you got anything they'd just give you a little, issued it out to you, just a little bit, not enough to even do you a month, and you'd just get it once a month. After you got fastened with them, they'd do what they wanted to do with you, because they knowed you wasn't going nowhere else—you didn't have no place to go. I know it's hard for y'all to understand these days what we did have to do on. I say, people wouldn't believe it unless they really had to live it. But it's true, dear, it is.

You worried all the time about where your next things was coming from. You had the children so you had to have clothes, you had to send them to school. It was just something to worry about all the time. You just didn't see your way. And there wasn't no jobs back then. After Floyd would get through with his little old crop—wasn't nothing to that— he'd get out and try to find a public working job, and the man would have to walk miles and miles to his work. Why yes, we was depressed, sure, we had to be.

That's why I thought he felt kindly sorry for us and the reason he done for us what he did. He and Walker'd go—they'd go sometimes and bring in stuff when I wouldn't even go with 'em. And then a lot of times they'd take me with them to Moundville to buy groceries for the children and anything the kids needed. Sure, we needed it, because we was all having it hard then. We wasn't the onliest ones that had it hard, you know. Everybody did at that time. And I wasn't ashamed of mine. Now, of course, we had plenty of vegetables and milk and butter and eggs and things like that, but they was other things that we went lacking for, and my kids did. I didn't have no right to even run them off.

We didn't believe that times would ever get any better with us; he was trying to encourage me that they would. He told me that I might not live to see it, but my children would have a better living than we was having then. But I couldn't believe it. But I'll have to say he was right, not that we're rich now, but one thing I can say is that they got

The Burroughs house interior. (Photos by Walker Evans)

their own homes, and they got a better living. They have anything they want near 'bout. He was right. I did live to see it. I don't know whether they had anything to do with it or not, but they had just been around and about, and they knowed what was coming, I guess, better than we did.

FROM Let Us Now Praise Famous Men

{A}ll that surrounded me, that silently strove in through my senses and stretched me full, was familiar and dear to me as nothing else on earth, and as if well known in a deep past and long years lost. . . . For half my blood is just this; and half my right of speech; and by blind chance alone is my life so softened and sophisticated. . . . And so in this quiet introit, and in all the time we have stayed in this house, and in all we have sought, and in each detail of it, there is so keen, sad, and precious a nostalgia as I can scarcely otherwise know; a knowledge of brief truancy into the sources of my life.

Ellie Mae Burroughs

I couldn't tell you the day they left. I know it was in the fall, 'cause we was gatherin' the crop in then, and they left and stayed gone; I thought they'd just slipped off, wasn't going to tell me about it. And then they come back one morning. They stayed gone about a week I guess and they come back. They told me now, they was gonna leave that time, but they just had to come back to see us. And I fixed their breakfast that mornin'. And while we was at the table they said, "Now we ain't going to tell you good-bye when we leave. We don't like to say good-bye. We'll just say so long, like we're coming back." I could've cried.

Elizabeth Tingle

They said they was leaving and wouldn't be back, and Mama's children cried; every one of us cried. They were so good to us, you know. They told us not to cry. "We'll be letting you hear from us," they said, which

The Burroughs house interior. (Photos by Walker Evans)

The Tingle Family. (Photo by Walker Evans)

they did do. But it kind of hurt Jim, you know, that crying. And Ruth told them, she said, "You're going to leave and ain't never gonna come back." She was real little then.

Robert Fitzgerald

I saw him as soon as he got back, of course, and I realized and we all realized that it had been, as one could have foreseen, a shaking kind of experience for him to take part as he had in these lives. Jim Agee was a Christian, and a profound one. And these were the lives of people who were, as one might say, the least of the Lord's people, so deep was their poverty and so hopeless was their life and their lot. And he had gone down from relative security and relative comfort to face all this. And as a Christian and as the man that he was, he couldn't have failed to feel that not only he, but the whole society that he'd gone as a representative of, was profoundly lacking to permit this kind of life to go on in those places.

He kept in touch with those people for years, sent them gifts for Christmas, those families, whom he had known down there. And of course, the book we have was in his mind only the beginning. He would have gone on, and for some time did plan to go on, with further books, about this whole situation. The three tenant families was just the beginning in his mind.

Ellie Mae Burroughs

I think it was about three or four different Christmases after they left that they sent a big package back, and every child would have a present. I'd have one and Floyd would have one, and then they'd have us a check to buy other things. I guess they thought we needed it, and we did, and we appreciated it. But they said we wouldn't ever forget them when they left, you know. They even sent Floyd clothes, you know. They sent him pants and things, had 'em made—they got his measurements and all when they left. Everyone said, "Well, you won't never hear from 'em no more." But it wasn't long 'til Floyd got that package back and had them

The Burroughs house exterior. (Photo by Walker Evans)

pants and things in there that he wanted. And when they'd send the Christmas presents they'd send it to all three of the families; Daddy's and the Tingle's and ours. It was nice.

Father Flye

He went down to Alabama in 1936 and had that unforgettable experience. Many persons couldn't have done that; the people wouldn't have opened up to them. But he was that sort of person; that is, he hadn't a trace of anything like superciliousness, or patronage, or talking down to people, or that kind of thing. There would be many people who couldn't adapt that way. They would have had a sense of, well, this is a specimen of human life that I'm objectively looking at. He had a loathing of doing that. He would have felt, well, after all, these are my fellow human beings, and my father's people were country people, and I wonder if I'd be doing as well as these folks are if I'd been brought up as they have been. Just great appreciation of these fellow human beings and their struggles and their rituals and their heroism, and so on. He would have felt that toward them, and they would have felt, well, he seems like just one of us.

Of course, that continually runs through the book, his being obsessed almost with that feeling. He was intensely interested in that, feeling that he would like to present them and the human condition as well as he could. It was something he would never forget. He had a great sense of understanding of various aspects of human life, but these weeks would contribute to the deepening of that, I'm sure.

James Agee

1936

Dear Father Flye,

The trip was very hard, and certainly one of the best things that ever happened to me. Writing what we found is a different matter, impossible in any form *Fortune* can use.

Part 2

All Over Alabama,

the lamps are out. Every leaf drenches the touch; the spider's net is heavy. The roads lie there, with nothing to use them. The fields lie there, with nothing at work in them, neither man nor beast. The plow handles are wet, and the rails and the frogplates and the weeds between the ties: and not even the hurryings and the hoarse sorrows of a distant train, on other roads, is heard. —from *Let Us Now Praise Famous Men*

*I*t is small wonder that this apparently routine *Fortune* assignment turned out to be the most challenging and frustrating task
Agee ever had to confront. When he returned from Alabama with his
raw materials, he and his second wife, Alma, moved to a small town in
New Jersey, where he began to write, taking on, it seemed, not only
Alabama's injustices, but the whole world's. He had married Alma
Mailman in 1938, shortly after obtaining a divorce from Olivia. Alma
was a gifted musician, and she and her husband listened to jazz for
hours together. They continued the intense literary life Agee had
pursued during his first marriage—though the birth of their son, Joel,
in 1940 made some of their long evening conversational vigils with
friends more difficult, certainly, for Alma. In 1941 she left New York

City with her baby son for Mexico, where she met Bodo Uhse, a German writer. Soon thereafter she divorced Agee, married Uhse, and with the child, Joel, went to live in East Germany.

Meanwhile, Agee had finished *Let Us Now Praise Famous Men*, and was, of course, unsatisfied with the result. His efforts to describe what he saw were monumental—as if the college student who admired James Joyce hoped to make out of this southern scene what Joyce had done with Dublin. Agee was never satisfied with the result of this effort. It is safe to say that he ultimately surrendered a portion of his labored, intense, tormented prose and reluctantly allowed it to emerge as the book we now know as *Let Us Now Praise Famous Men*. Even to call it that, "a book," is to tread on Agee's sensitive toes: "This is a *book* only by necessity. More seriously, it is an effort in human actuality, in which the reader is no less centrally involved than the authors and those of whom they tell."

Agee was a great performer—a mimic, a scold, a man capable of large, defiant (and self-wounding) gestures. He had the dramatist's interest in others, the great audience of readers whom he never ignored. He wanted from his readers a kind of engagement worthy of his own high standards; he was willing to take big risks in order to get such a level of attention. *Let Us Now Praise Famous Men* can be regarded as a moral drama, a long prose-poem structured as a presentation. We begin with "Persons and Places," a *dramatis personae* of sorts. There are "Verses," a "Preamble," a quotation from *King Lear*, a section called "Intermission: Conversation in the Lobby," and a section described as "Inductions." The author wants to tell us about those concrete essentials of our lives, money and shelter and clothing and education and work, but he is constantly searching for ways to turn such "topics" into an edifying spectacle, with protagonists, confrontations, rising action, a compelling denouement or two—in hopes that we as viewers, strongly "involved," won't smugly close the covers of "yet another book." Agee's chief enemy was the same as that of every ambitious moral writer—the potential boredom of the proudly well-intentioned reader, for whom *Let Us Now Praise Famous Men* would be regarded as providing a good, vivid account of a "problem," that is 1930s southern tenantry.

Agee begins his book by offering a footnote to explain his reasons for putting lines from *King Lear* ("Poor naked wretches, whereso'er you are, / That bide the pelting of this pitiless storm,") on one opening page, and on an opposite page, the well-known political exhortation that begins with "Workers of the world, unite and fight." Agee's explanation of his resort to these two statements tells a lot about what he has in mind for his book, and reveals in full display the many (and seemingly conflicting) sides of his writing personality. He begins provocatively, if not with condescending resignation: "These words are quoted here to mislead those who will be misled by them. They mean, not what the reader may come to think they mean, but what they say." The author is fighting hard an inclination in all of us (certainly including himself) to let urgency slip—to bury the terribly demanding significance of a given message in, of all ironies, our capacity for recognition.

"Expose thyself to feel what wretches feel" is a line (a bit further along) of the above-mentioned Shakespeare quote. So many of us are capable of "enjoying" such lines of that play, even memorizing whole sections of its poetry—thereby, it can be said, protecting ourselves from the terrible burden, the enormous ethical challenge being put to us. We all know that once there was a writer, born in Stratford-on-Avon; and out of his heart and soul came words he summoned with unforgettable grace and precision, ideas he wanted us to consider, and notions of what this life means and how it ought to be lived. In no time, however, we take him and make "play," so to speak—bury him in memorized lines, in pedantic readings and counter-readings, in an assortment of interpretations that concentrate our attention so closely we lose sight of the overall directions suggested by a bold and inspired visionary. The result is the blindness of the sighted, no matter their education. This is *Lear*, we nod, and recall the scene, the act. This is a communist rallying cry, we nod, and think of Marx and Engels, of Leninism-Stalinism, of revolutions won, then badly betrayed.

Agee wants to reclaim spirited, thoughtful compassion from both academic pedants and political tyrants. He is, he tells us, singing. He refers in his footnote to "the sonata form." He is addressing questions of justice, of fate, even as playwrights from the beginning of (our) time have done so—Sophocles and Euripides, and then Shakespeare. Why do some live so well, while others starve? Why do Christians forget Christ's words, His very life? And as the Greeks wondered before Him, what does suffering do to people, not only to the sufferers themselves, but to the rest of us, witnesses in greater jeopardy than we (mostly) want to realize?

But there is, as in the sonata, a second voice; Agee had visited three families, after all, and he had noticed the manner in which they tried, collectively and against high odds indeed, to get through one day, then another. He may have romanticized their lives somewhat, expressed one time too many his admiration for their pluck, and forsaken, except in a few passages, an analysis of the mean and brutish inclinations to be found among the poor as well as the rich and well-born. But he was convinced, as others have been (one thinks of Oscar Lewis, of Studs Terkel), that there is something communal about this life that even dire poverty or political repression don't obliterate. "We are at our wit's end; we are down and out, real bad down and out; but we are we"—I once heard it put by a migrant farm worker, a woman who had been drinking and who, even sober, was somewhat at loose ends psychologically, not to mention socially and economically, but a woman, too, who wanted to look beyond herself, toward others, related by blood and related by condition. And a woman who wanted to *do* something—enlist the long fearful, the intimidated, and the acquiescent into a specific, concerted struggle; a struggle against "chains," as in "You have nothing to lose but your chains." After all, our own government had gone into federal court, in Florida, charging "peonage"—in the 1970s, almost a half-century after Agee had visited Alabama.

Agee completes the footnote mentioned above with an admonition; he worries about the "tendency to label" in all of us, no matter our effort to avoid doing so, and so he insists that "neither these words [Workers of the world . . .] nor the authors are property of any political party, faith, or faction." The writer is, to be sure, giving us a conventional warning— of a kind a writer, especially, would want to offer: Try to heed these quoted words (and mine, too) with an open mind, uncluttered by all the deadening, distorting associations to which we are all heir. On the other hand, Agee must have known that some of those associations are not frivolous or mean-spirited or stupid, but rather come from our history (from our collective experience), and have lessons to teach us. Even as there are "famous men" who have been like the people Agee saw in Alabama (unnoticed, humble, in constant danger of illness, malnutrition, and complete economic ruin), so there are "famous men" who *have* tried to "unite and fight," and who have not lost their chains, but found new ones—like those in the Gulag, for instance.

In the 1930s, long before many others among our so-called intelligentsia, Agee was skeptical of Stalinist or Trotskyite sectarianism; he knew that not only "words" end up becoming the "property" of this or that "political party, faith, or faction," but thousands and thousands of innocent, honorable lives as well. Yet, he felt the sensitive observer's indignation—an exact and fitting response to the indignity he couldn't stop himself from noticing. He had, in his own fashion, read *Lear* carefully, and he had risked his own kind of "exposure." Now he wondered, in the words of V. I. Lenin, "What is to be done?" Agee knew that Lenin ought to have asked that question a second time around, so to speak, from within the walls of his Kremlin office. Agee's dilemma was that of the revolutionary post-revolutionary, the one who has seen a decent hope crushed by traitors, by evil, by blind submission to arrogant dogma, and on and on. Nor is the dilemma only of this century, as Agee the Christian (in spirit) well knew, contemplating the travesty of so much that has happened in the name of "Christianity."

Of course, Agee wasn't only protecting "these words" from the domination of one or another "party, faith, or faction." He was aiming to guard himself as well. He was, so often, emotionally anarchic—caught in various binds which, collectively, seemed at times about to tear him apart. He was also anarchic in the social scene—quick (too quick, some felt) to take issue with mere conventions, thereby granting them, ironically, more weight and importance than they might otherwise have possessed. And he was, moreover, an anarchist in the broadest sense—though not in the specific political sense. That is, he assumed the right to his own critical posture as a writer, as he viewed rural Alabama in 1936, and, later, the rest of America and other parts of the world.

He had plenty of doubt and sarcasm to hand out, and one gets the impression that no political party, no idea become a "movement," would ever be immune from the skeptical part of his mind. The danger is captiousness—a chronic insistence, all-or-none fashion, that political leaders or social movements (or writers, for that matter), either pass full muster or be subjected to withering and continual criticism. At times Agee fell victim to such a posture, turning, for instance, with ironic bitterness, or snide contempt, or outright scorn, on a wide spectrum of subjects: Franklin D. Roosevelt and his New Deal; the teachers of the rural South, black and white alike; or New York intellectuals. Even the "reader," a catchall designation if there ever was one, gets hit by a swipe or two—by, of all people, a writer who worries about "the average reader's tendency to label." A provoked reader, not at all content to be called "average," might at the very least remind the author that he shows evidence of having been a "reader" himself, and, as a matter of fact, in a long prose section of *Permit Me Voyage*, seemed quite ready to dish out a few labels himself.

But Agee was nothing if not self-critical. He knew the "reader" in himself, and also the reactively humble writer, still unable to lick decisively the sin of sins: pride. Much of the tension in *Let Us Now Praise Famous Men* stems from an internal duet, so to speak—two different aspects of Agee's sensibility trying to construct for the listener (shall we now say?), "average" or otherwise, a reasonably coherent and sustained lyrical composition. Those who remember the Augustinian "confessions" of one or another college course will have no difficulty seeing, at the very minimum, one of those "historical continuities" we sometimes hear about worked into the following substantial (in several senses of the word) sentence, put to the reader at the start of the book, just when he or she thinks himself or herself past a few curve balls, if not hand grenades:

> *It seems to me curious, not to say obscene and thoroughly terrifying, that it could occur to an association of human beings drawn together through need and chance and for profit into a company, an organ of journalism, to pry intimately into the lives of an undefended and appallingly damaged group of human beings, an ignorant and helpless rural family, for the purpose of parading the nakedness, disadvantage and humiliation of these lives before another group of human beings, in the name of science, of "honest journalism" (whatever that paradox may mean), of humanity, of*

social fearlessness, for money, and for a reputation for crusading and for unbias which, when skillfully enough qualified, is exchangeable at any bank for money (and in politics, for votes, job patronage, abelincolnism, etc.); and that these people could be capable of meditating this prospect without the slightest doubt of their qualification to do an "honest" piece of work, and with a conscience better than clear, and in the virtual certitude of almost unanimous public approval.

Little is left, one begins to feel. We are all suspect after such an assault, all the readers and all the writers and all the editors of all the magazines and publishing houses—all of us who are, finally, human beings, and who have our blind spots, and our self-centeredness, and our wish to live in comfort and with some approval from others, and who write out of egoism and vanity or in a desperate outcry of preachiness meant for our own ears more than anyone else's, and who are indulgent with ourselves in dozens of ways, and who certainly struggle with ironies and paradoxes galore, including the terrible ones that the more we expose and denounce the blatant evils of this world, the more we become a prominent part of the very world in which that evil seems to flourish, and so we get rewarded and become (speaking of ironies) "famous men" because we have highlighted the lives of a "them" (even if called "famous men"), and so it goes, as a writer who once went to St. Andrew's School in Sewanee, Tennessee would not be averse to putting it, "world without end."

Moreover, such self-criticism does not entitle one to any guarantee of absolution. Mea culpas can be a sly form of arrogance, or a canny means of currying favor—the reader's sympathy enlisted on behalf of an earnestly disarming breast-beater, who turns out to be, in the clutch, quite capable of a cleverly effective self-defense. But Agee wasn't only taking on himself in the old monkish tradition of endless, excoriating introspection. He spells out what he considers to be "curious, obscene, terrifying and unfathomly mysterious" in a sentence that bears quoting here—as an example of his thinking, surely, but also as an example of the kind of sonorous, suggestive, baffling, cranky prose he could mobilize and put in the "average reader's" way:

So does the whole subsequent course and fate of the work: the causes for its non-publication, the details of its later acceptance elsewhere, and of its design; the problems which confronted the maker of the photographs; and those which confront me as I try to write of it: the question, Who are you who will read these words and study these photographs, and through what cause, by what chance, and for what purpose, and by what right do you qualify to, and what will you do about it; and the question, Why we make this book, and set it at large, and by what right, and for what purpose, and to what good end, or none: the whole memory of the South in its six-thousand-mile parade and flowering outlay of the façades of cities, and of the eyes in the streets of towns, and of hotels, and of the trembling heat, and of the wide wild opening of the tragic land, wearing the trapped frail flowers of its garden of faces; the fleet flush and flower and fainting of the human crop it raises; the virulent, insolent, deceitful, pitying, infinitesimal and frenzied running and searching, on this colossal peasant map, of two angry, futile and bottomless, botched and overcomplicated youthful intelligences in the service of an anger and of a love and of an undiscernible truth, and in the frightening vanity of their would-be purity; the sustaining, even now, and forward moving, lifted on the lifting of this day as ships on a wave, above whom, in a few hours, night once more will stand up in his stars, and they decline through lamplight and be dreaming statues, of those, each, whose lives we knew and whom we love and intend well toward, and of whose living we know little in some while now, save that quite steadily, in not much possible change for better or much worse, mute, innocent, helpless and incorporate among that small-moted and inestimable swarm and pollen stream and fleet of single, irreparable, unrepeatable existences, they are led, gently, quite steadily, quite without mercy, each a little farther toward the washing and the wailing, the sunday suit and the prettiest dress, the pine box, and the closed clay room whose fraily decorated roof, until rain has taken it flat into oblivion, wears the shape of a ritual scar and of an inverted boat: curious, obscene, terrifying, beyond all search of dream unanswerable, those problems which stand thickly forth like light from all matter, triviality, chance, intention, and record in the body, of being, of truth, of conscience, of hope, of hatred, of beauty, of indignation, of guilt, of betrayal, of innocence, of forgiveness, of vengeance, of guardianship, of an indenominable fate, predicament, destination, and God.

It is no small relief, after that paragraph of a sentence, to come up with, immediately afterward, the following: "Therefore it is in some fear that I approach those matters at all, and in much confusion." The "average reader," upon acquaintance with that last noun, sighs and nods affirmatively. But what is Agee's intent here? He is, perhaps, trying to make his "confusion" as contagious as it turns out, often enough, to be. I have used this book in my courses, and have heard the "confusion" expressed vigorously: sincere annoyance, plaintive cries for interpretive assistance, angry shrugs of the shoulders, or straightforward contempt. It is hard not only to get through his prose, but to emerge without feeling some strong emotion. Nor is the teacher always grateful for the student who worships ecstatically Agee's writing, his various postures. There is to his writing the quality of transcendence: a great, dramatic, daring lift upward—away from all the petty, self-serving, uncritical ones who live on campuses or in various commercial offices. And he can disarm one utterly with the sweetness of his talk, the compelling evocation of a complex kind of compassion. But he is also a very angry writer, and surely he wants an engagement of sorts with us, a willingness on our part to say no, to say stop, to say, even, *basta!*, enough!

Agee has asked of himself, in this book, that he walk a long tightrope. He can be seen at many points to be wavering, even tottering. His inconsistencies, if not contradictions, are worthy of the novelist, trying with all his might to imitate life. At times he walks along surely, wondrously, the fine poet turning out marvelous descriptions of people, places, events. His lyrical gifts show themselves over and over again— touching, even stunning, moments in which the ordinary (the earth, flowers, furniture, buildings) is made, miraculously, to reveal the divine. "Behind the house," we are told, "the dirt is blond and bare, except a little fledgling of grass-leaves at the roots of structures, and walked-out rags of grass thickening along the sides." As for the pine wood of those tenant farmer cabins, if not shacks: "In some of this wood, the grain is broad and distinct: in some of it the grain has almost disappeared, and the wood has a texture and look like that of weathered bone." And then there are those other buildings: "The henroost is about seven feet square and five high, roofed with rotted shingles. It is built rather at random of planks varying in width between a foot and four inches, nailed on horizontally with narrow spaces between their edges." We learn more than the above about that henroost—wonderful, carefully presented details of structure and function, including the marvelous, wry observation that "most of the eggs are found by the children in places which are of the hens' own selection."

On the other hand, Agee has by no means contented himself with close, pastoral cataloging; or even, with the good storytelling that he as a novelist could manage—as when he turns a sleepless night into the hellish experience it was, with a hot, sweaty, city-spoiled visitor struggling desperately to deal with bugs and ticks and flies and mosquitoes. We are tested in many ways, and sometimes the small ordeals are the most revealing about our hopes and fears. Agee proves he knows this on page after page—and the result is a successful challenge to reality by a writer: We get to know some Alabama people of the 1930s "right well," as they might have put it. But there are other pages, and they are, as critics sometimes put it, more "problematical." A section titled "Education," for instance, presents the author as a social critic with a vengeance. Nor is that last noun merely a rhetorical flourish. Agee's anger is boundless in that chapter, and spills from Alabama to just about everywhere. And shaking his fists hard and often, he naturally risks losing his grip on logic.

He makes clear, for instance, the deficiencies of a particular Alabama county school system. He quotes from the books used, then expresses freely his scorn: "Personally I see enough there [in the various educational matters he has examined] to furnish me with bile for a month." His point of view, actually, is prophetic; long before Paul Goodman, Agee was alert to the banality, if not stupidity, that passes for "instructional materials" in many schools. He even goes after the school buildings he saw, describing one as "a recently built, windowy, 'healthful' red brick and white-trimmed new structure which perfectly exemplifies the American genius for sterility, unimagination, and general gutlessness. . . ." That was a *white* school, one hastens to add. As for the *other* school: "The negro children, meanwhile, continue to sardine themselves, a hundred and a hundred and twenty strong, into stove-heated one-room pine shacks which might comfortably accommodate a fifth of their number if the walls, roof, and windows were tight."

What, precisely, would Agee have wanted for such children, in the way of books, teaching, buildings? In the course of a criticism of Alabama "education," he blasts *all* education—including his own. He tells us this: "I could not wish of any one of them [the children he has met down South] that they should have had the 'advantages' I have had: a Harvard education is by no means an unqualified advantage." What are such bold pronouncements supposed to mean? It is all right for James Agee, Harvard '32, well-paid writer, Alabama visitor, to decry universities, those who teach in them ("few doctors of philosophy are literate"), and one or another educational "establishment." Are the Alabama children he met to pay heed, however? Would he really tell one of them to stay clear of scholarships offered to a given school, a given college, on the ground that a good deal of hypocrisy and pretense go on in such places, *among others?*

Nowhere is Agee's rock-bottom philosophical and psychological romanticism more evident than in *Let Us Now Praise Famous Men,* and especially in his analysis of "education." He anticipates not only Paul Goodman, but R. D. Laing: "As a whole part of 'psychological education' it needs to be remembered that a neurosis can be valuable; also that 'adjustment' to a sick and insane environment is of itself not 'health' but sickness and insanity." Maybe that is so familiar as to be trite, these days—when there are more than enough individuals willing to celebrate various kinds of eccentric behavior, if not madness itself. But when Agee was writing the above words, psychoanalysis was just making itself felt as a strong presence in the relatively well-to-do intellectual circles to which Agee and Evans belonged. The point, at the time, was to conquer neurosis, through analytic treatment. There was a good deal of hopefulness, even fatuous conviction among such "analysands," not to mention their doctors—that a new kind of person would emerge, no longer heir to the various conflicts others keep having. Anna Freud, in *Normality and Pathology* (1965) has documented rather compellingly what came to be a sectarian, messianic ("prophylactic") movement of sorts. For Agee to have resisted such a line of thinking, even to have seen that there is a social and cultural aspect to psychiatric nomenclature (it can be used to put people down, and alas, as a justification for locking them up in order to silence their unpopular voices) was to indicate a certain stubborn independence of mind, as well as a shrewd capacity to puncture a given kind of faddish illusion.

Yet, at other moments he can spin his own illusions, earnestly well-intentioned as he is: "I don't know whether negroes or whites teach in the negro schools; I presume negroes. If they are negroes, I would presume for general reasons that many of them, or most, are far superior to the white teachers." I fear the man who shuns categorical approximations and gratuitous labeling proves himself not immune to the practice. To be sure, he indicates his reasons; whites can get better jobs, whereas for a black to be a schoolteacher is to be at the top, hence "many of the most serious and intelligent negroes become teachers." But apart from the fact that in the 1930s it wasn't so easy for whites, no matter their abilities, to get very good jobs, in Alabama or elsewhere, some of us who have worked in schools in the rural South or in the North have not found race to be so definitively correlated with teaching excellence. Agee knows about, and even refers to, "the Uncle Tom attitude," which was certainly in the 1930s a terrible necessity, it seemed, for blacks working under segregationist authorities. Yet, I have seen black teachers in Alabama show other unfortunate "attitudes"—meanness and narrowness, the very attributes Agee seems ready to lay exclusively at the door of white teachers, maybe even a few who teach at Ivy League colleges.

I suppose I am circling a particular bush—that of liberal *and* radical sentimentality. Agee tells us, at one point, that " 'Education' as it stands is tied in with every bondage" he can think of; he goes on to say that it "is the chief cause of these bondages. . . ." Mere rhetoric, one suspects—or a bloated version of what education is, and does, and is able to do. Agee himself claimed to have learned rather a lot at St. Andrew's, at Exeter, at Harvard—from teachers whom he mentions with considerable thankfulness and praise in *Permit Me Voyage*. He came to Alabama a thoroughly educated young man, no matter the flaws in the schools he attended. The families he visited in the South don't quite need the kind of burden he places on them—virtuous innocents, who ought be protected from the corruptions of something called "Education." Nor do they need their human dignity used as a foil by one of a relative handful lucky enough during the Depression to be able to obtain an Exeter and Harvard education.

When that college graduate, so literate himself, takes up the subject of literacy, he makes it hard for anyone to figure out what should be done in Alabama or in the rest of the United States. He declares scornfully that "literacy" is "a pleasing word." Why shouldn't that be so? Well, the supposedly educated aren't very smart. As for the tenant farmers we've been learning about, they may have a lot of trouble reading or spelling or writing, never mind "critically examining . . . any 'ideas,' whether true or false." But know this: "That they are, by virtue of these limitations, among the only 'honest' and 'beautiful' users of language, is true, perhaps, but it is not enough." As if that paradox weren't itself "enough," we are reminded immediately that such people are "at an immeasurable disadvantage in a world which is run, and in which they are hurt, and in which they might be cured, by 'knowledge' and by 'ideas.' " And as if *that* weren't a bit hard to digest, the following quite categorical assertion is made: "[A]nd to 'consciousness' or 'knowledge' in its usages in personal conduct and in human relationships, and to those unlimited worlds of the senses, the remembrance, the mind and the heart which, beyond that of their own existence, are the only human hope, dignity, solace, increasement, and joy, they are all but totally blinded."

The mind boggles at the prospect of trying to sort out the various lines of reasoning, the various assumptions that prompt such statements—and there are dozens of others of a similarly stunning nature. Agee loved the people he met. He also felt, and acknowledged feeling, terribly guilty while with them, because he was the lucky, privileged outsider, soon enough to be back in Manhattan, playing Beethoven's Ninth Symphony in a room with a majestic view of—well, New York City's ghettoes, as a matter of fact, among other things. He wanted to hold up his new (temporary) friends as honorable and decent men, women, children. But he was with them rather briefly—and surely there was an element of restraint on all sides, as hosts and guests fumbled toward some reasonable trust. Still, one doubts Agee saw and heard all there was to see and hear—and he knew, of course, that such was the case. In a year, in two years, there still might have been secrets not discovered—though as a rule the more time people spend together, the better they get to know each other. The point is that Agee spent much less time than he knew would be a reasonably adequate span—and that fact only added to his already high quota of self-recrimination, bordering on self-flagellation.

As one goes through *Let Us Now Praise Famous Men*, one begins to notice that the above-described responses and conclusions lead the writer, unsurprisingly, to the edge of despair, if not to its very center. What to do, psychologically? I do not mean "psychologically" in any *clinical* sense. I do not mean to get into an analysis of James Agee's complex mental life and its bearing upon his work; quite frankly, I believe such an effort directed at any writer's life produces a low yield of useful information and a large quantity of that which is fairly banal. Everyone's mental life, plumbed deep and wide, turns out to be complex. Millions of us have been hurt or made to feel vulnerable or especially sensitive—yet don't find ourselves able or willing to wrestle with words, as Agee did so very successfully. The point is not Agee's "childhood" as a putative source of later literary productivity, nor Agee's "psychopathology" (which we all have, in one form or another) as an "explanation" of later interests, attitudes, involvements. The point, rather, is that Agee's sort of mission is bound to push the mind hard. If we are, that is, to follow Shakespeare's advice, and that of those nineteenth-century political revolutionaries who wanted to overthrow various despots (leaving aside what history would give us as the consequence), then we had better be prepared to deal with the moral anger that goes along, side by side, with such moral analysis—namely, the kind meant to prompt social change. And anger craves objects.

Agee is continually self-lacerating, but he rouses himself, at critical times, to a fierce assault on a wide range of others, some rather surprising. In the section "Money," he begins with a remark Franklin Delano Roosevelt made during one of his campaigns: "You are farmers; I am a farmer myself." We then are yanked down to Alabama to learn about the finances of some impossibly poor farmers with whom the squire of New York State's Hyde Park, overlooking the Hudson River, has declared an occupational solidarity. The effect, of course, is achieved: devastating irony. The reader is brought up short, confronted through the disarming use of a quotation with all sorts of uncomfortable facts and thoughts—not least, the glibness of liberal rhetoric, once viewed from a certain vantage point. "What is one to do?" one cries. Did not Roosevelt try hard, extremely hard, all during the 1930s, and against great opposition, to alleviate the distress of America's poor farm people? If the mental and moral life of tenant farmers is worth painstaking consideration, as in *Let Us Now Praise Famous Men*, are we to dismiss the political struggle of the 1930s waged by Franklin Delano Roosevelt, among others, with a cleverly placed quotation of his, taken utterly out of the context of a given speech, made during one particular campaign? And if the worst charge has to be leveled at Agee—that he delivered a cheap shot—then what is to be said in defense of it?

He would, no doubt, laugh if not sneer at such a series of questions. He was a writer, responding as such to a given set of circumstances—making all sorts of connections, symbolic and quite literal, in hopes of setting other minds in motion, even as his mind had been awakened, moved to cry, to sing, to perform. If a line or two spoken by an American president in the 1930s struck Agee's fancy, so to speak, as he contemplated rural Alabama, then so be it. The job of the poet, the novelist, and at least some literary essayists is not detailed political analysis (either with respect to farm labor or reformist national politics), nor, for that matter, psychiatric analysis; and not necessarily cool, documentary exposition or logical argument. I had the privilege of knowing, when in medical school, William Carlos Williams, like Agee a poet and novelist who had a strong interest in social and political matters from which he couldn't keep away, despite the strong intuition on his part that he spoke subjectively, and not rarely went awry in his judgments. Once he said to me: "I sound off, sometimes—and strike out. But even so, I think I strike out making a lot of noise, and catching the attention of some people, and if it's an issue that's important, and they stop and think what *they* think, I'm glad." Perhaps Agee wouldn't mind associating himself with Dr. Williams's candid acknowledgment, if not justification.

Not that Agee didn't come up with his own rather vigorous, if not stark and grim and surprising, explanation of what he was about—an apology of sorts for an occasional misstep:

> *I am not at all trying to lay out a thesis, far less to substantiate or to solve. I do not consider myself qualified. I know only that murder is being done, against nearly every individual in the planet, and that there are dimensions and correlations of cure which not only are not being used but appear to be scarcely considered or suspected. I know there is cure, even now available, if only it were available, in science and in the fear and joy of God. This is only a brief personal statement of these convictions: and my self-disgust is less in my ignorance, and far less in my "failure" to "defend" or "support" the statement, than in my inability to state it even so far as I see it, and in my inability to blow out the brains with it of you who take what it is talking of lightly, or not seriously enough.*

He is writing, then, in a non-academic tradition, even an anti-academic one. He does not advertise himself as a "field worker," certainly not a social scientist. He is not, either, a journalist reporting in the factual or muckraking traditions—or, at least, not *only* such a writer. There are, definitely, reportorial aspects to the book. But this is the book, mainly, of an unashamed moralist, who happens, also, to be a marvelously exact and discerning employer of words. It is the book, too, as the above passage indicates, of a mind reared in twentieth-century technological hope—edged, however, by a lingering Christian vision, not at all triumphant, yet not acknowledged with mere lip-service, either. There are, once again, the strenuous assaults on the author's own worth, a bit startling in the context of his membership in an intelligentsia more apt to turn to others critically—or define the tendency to do so with oneself as evidence of psychological illness. For Agee, the "self-disgust" mentioned in his confessional outcry connects, one keeps feeling, with St. Augustine and St. John of the Cross and Pascal—a Christian critical self-scrutiny that will not yield, even today, its dignity to the claims of those who use words such as *masochism* or *depression*.

As for the regret on the author's part that he hasn't quite been able to "blow out the brains" of various readers with the truculent assertions he has worked into a deliberately discordant and unwieldy book, we are not wise to ignore the remark as a foolish and regrettable instance of hyperbole. "Agee's rebellion," Walker Evans insisted from the retrospective vantage point of 1960, "was unquenchable, self-damaging, deeply principled, infinitely costly, and ultimately priceless." The "principled" voice of Agee's was not shed easily; it sets the tone for a lot of his writing—and certainly, the "rebellion" Evans mentions was part of a particular religious tradition. The Judeo-Christian "principles," after all, which prompted such dedicated rage in Agee were stated first by an angry Jeremiah, an angry Isaiah, and, in the New Testament, by a Jesus suddenly not so meek and accepting, but full of scorn and disgust as he confronts the arid pietism of the Temple.

When Agee talks of "murder," he is once more flirting with hyperbole, many of us have a right to think—and when he says that this "murder" is being committed "against nearly every individual in the planet," we may well ask precisely what the author means. Who is doing the killing, and with what in mind? And when we are told that a "cure" is available, but is not being "considered or suspected," we are at a bit of a logical impasse. The verb *consider* leads down one road, the verb *suspect* down quite another. There are, here, issues of will and availability and responsibility and possibility—all thrown into a boiling, moralistic stew. Can one consider what is not suspected? Or is the author referring to the workings of the unconscious—our ability not to consider, not even to suspect, when we are indisposed to do so by virtue of the mind's ability to blot from awareness certain matters?

There is, further, the enigmatic statement of Agee's that he knows "there is a cure." Or is there one? The qualifying expression ("if only it were available") rendered as a conditional clause of hope, makes one wonder, yet again, what Agee is really thinking. But soon enough he summons the phrase "personal statement," as if any of his readers had by now, page 307 of his book, any substantial doubts. The final thrust, about wanting "to blow out the brains" of the reader, reminds one, not for the first time, that R. D. Laing, who used a similar phrase with respect to *his* readers, did not in the 1960s break as much new ground as some of his followers may have believed.

Moreover, to go a further mile, critically, we must contend with the preacher who demands of his audience that they not take a given message or problem presented "lightly," or with insufficient seriousness. Who is to make these calibrations, using what criteria? What does the author want—empathy stated, sympathy and understanding shouted from all available rooftops? A stint of time spent in Alabama, in an effort to "help" others with their various "problems"? How long a spell, as a matter of fact—especially since Agee himself was gone in August 1936, having arrived in July 1936? And doing what: teaching in schools the author condemns so bitterly, or helping in the fields, when no help is really required? Cash—is that the answer, a philanthropic inundation? Maybe the people Agee knew would have answered yes to that last question, and with undisguised, unmodified enthusiasm. But one wonders what pitch of skeptical scorn might have been forthcoming, thereupon, from a writer who had such contempt for the material side of American capitalism—while at the same time living off it, as a writer, and before that as a student at a wealthy school and an even wealthier college.

The question persists, therefore: What kind of seriousness did the author have in mind for us—if he is not to shoot us through the head? I fear there is no clear answer forthcoming. There remains, inevitably, the reader's sense that he or she is being hit hard with rhetoric, and the best thing to do is proceed—turn the pages, hoping for a further acquaintance with Alabama's people, or, to be candid, in the thrilled expectation of a few more jabs.

When *Let Us Now Praise Famous Men* reappeared in 1960 an altogether different climate of opinion had evolved. In the generally prosperous late 1950s the most visible and urgent problems were the racial conflict and severe, unremitting rural poverty of the South, which had not shared in the social and economic improvements other Americans had come to take for granted. In 1954 the Supreme Court sent a strong signal to the South, with a decision declaring school segregation to be unconstitutional. In 1956 President Eisenhower sent in federal troops. By 1957 Rosa Parks had taken her stand in Montgomery, Alabama— saying *enough!* to segregationist laws that told the people where to sit, stand, eat, learn. A hitherto unknown minister, Dr. Martin Luther King, Jr., was quickly at Rosa Parks's side, and quickly became an important leader. In 1960 an election gave us the youngest president in history, ready and willing to bring new energy to our political life. A sudden tide of social change, the civil rights movement, was rising dramatically by 1960. How timely and enterprising of Houghton Mifflin at that point to give the public, a whole new generation of Americans, a chance to meet James Agee and Walker Evans and the people whose lives they'd chronicled a quarter of a century earlier. It was a perfect insight into an obscure part of the nation, a region which, for so many of us, had remained hidden in a unique kind of obscurity, seemingly obsessed with a mythic past, terribly reluctant to say good-bye to laws and social habits that were now regarded by the rest of the country as a national disgrace.

I remember buying *Let Us Now Praise Famous Men* and seeing many others do so. I remember finding copies of the book, hardcover no less, all over the South, especially in Freedom Houses, as we called them back in the summer of 1964 during the voter-registration projects in the steadfastly segregationist Delta. In Canton, Mississippi, in Greenwood, Mississippi, in Yazoo City, Mississippi—on a table, on the floor, on a bed, on a chair, read by white, well-to-do students from Ivy League colleges, and read, as well, by black students from the North and from the South. A bible of sorts, at that time—a sign, a symbol, a reminder, an eloquent testimony that others had cared, had gone forth to look and hear, and had come back, stood up, and addressed their friends, their neighbors, and the entire nation. It was a talisman for so many of those young civil rights activists—such as this one: "I hold on to that book; I'm afraid to lose it. Why? Because it's as if I have a very close friend here, and he's gone through a lot of the confusions I'm going through, and he's put it all down, so when I feel like throwing in the towel, I pick up that book of Agee's, and I read over and over one of his incredible pages, the long paragraphs, the torment, the flood of words, buoying you up, though, not drowning you. I get embarrassed at times, by his honesty; he makes you realize how troubled you are, and how troubling everything is, because he was brave and honest enough to expose himself, and show us how mixed up he was.

98

"I don't mean *psychiatrically* mixed up; you're wrong, if that's what you think—or think I think! I mean mixed up the way life is mixed up! I went to Harvard, like Agee. I went to Andover, not Exeter; big difference! This is July, the same month those two went South. It's only a short ride from here and you're in Alabama. I'll be leaving in September to go back to Cambridge, to Harvard Law School, about the same thing as returning to Manhattan, so you can pick up paychecks from Henry R. Luce and his hired hands. I think of Agee so often I guess I'd have to call him a close buddy of mine, even if he's dead. He knew all the crazy contradictions we live with these days. He wanted to help others, but he had a career as a writer—meaning he wanted to help himself! He knew that a lot of the stuff you read about, the stuff people believe, the latest 'ideas'—they're all pretty shallow, and won't last. But he couldn't really get down on his knees and pray to God Almighty, the way my grandparents do, in their nice suburban Episcopalian church! He was a good person—he knew that, even though he gives himself a lousy time every second or third page in the book; but he was also selfish, like we all are, and it hurt him, I guess, to know so much about himself and to want to be a help to others, and to feel for them and be able to immerse himself in them, but then to pull back and think of James Agee, and what he wants to write, and his life up in exciting mid-Manhattan and the Village, the parties and the plays and concerts and the films he loved to see, the literary life and the literary gossip, and all the rest of the charmed things that make it so great to be alive, for him and others like him, me included.

"Maybe we're hypocrites. That's what he's really fighting—the voice inside himself that calls him a phony, and that tells him either to shut up and get down to work in Alabama (or in New York), work hard and work long for the poor, or stop hollering at everyone else. I mean, is it enough to call other people, the poor and the humble, 'famous men,' but then keep plugging at becoming the kind of 'famous man' Agee was, when he died, the kind of 'famous men' our Ivy League schools keep boasting of as their graduates! I wouldn't even know how to answer that question! I don't know what I'll be like even next year, never mind when I'm as old as Agee was when he published *Let Us Now Praise Famous Men*. He was just over thirty, I believe—and still struggling. Hell, he only had fifteen years to go, and he'd be dead. Some of us die a lot earlier—I mean, we're technically alive, but we're dead."

Other students, black, responded to quite different aspects of Agee's book, and of course, to different sides of Agee himself, the person who so evidently and provocatively inhabits the book. At first I often wondered why some of the blacks I knew in SNCC (the Student Non-Violent Coordinating Committee, a major organization involved in the civil rights struggle of the early 1960s) had such favorable words for Agee's books. True, they also had strong reservations, which grew stronger as they themselves withdrew increasingly from a cooperative effort with whites into the insistent "black power" position. But here is how a black youth from Tuscaloosa (not all that far from the Alabama territory Agee stalked) explained his feelings about "*the* book," as he kept calling it: "There's no book like it, at least that I've seen. It's *the* book—the one book where a white man lets it all hang out, and he's not trying to kid himself, and he doesn't let you and me, reading him, pull all kinds of tricks. I mean, this guy is honest! He may be troubled, but that's the truth of his life and everyone else's, that we've got a lot of trouble. Like he says, if you're *not* troubled by all the trouble, big trouble, we have in this country—well, then, you're *really* in trouble, big trouble.

"To me, the proof of the truth in Agee's writing is that he makes mistakes, big ones. I mean, for a black, the big moment is in that small section called 'Near a Church,' where he's with his buddy Walker Evans, I believe, and they're getting the camera set up, and they see a Negro couple, and I guess Evans wanted to photograph them, but whatever the couple had on their minds, Agee was walking behind them, and he disturbed them. They heard him and looked, and he got closer, and they froze, they just froze: Who is this white guy, and what in hell is he going to do to us? Pretty fast, Agee sees the whole lousy situation: the young Negro couple, scared to death, and he wanting to be nice and friendly, but knowing there was no way, no way, not even for him, big and easy with words, to dissolve the crazy, terrible stuff that was going on between 'them' and him and his buddy. The two young Negroes stare at him. They just stare. I guess he stared back. Talk about fear!

"We see that same fear today here, doing our organizing. I'm black, and *I* scare the people here, because I'm an outsider. They don't know what I want. They can't get a fix on me. Anyway, Agee saw the whole horrible story of 'race relations' in the South in those few seconds, and he tells you how he felt—as rotten and no good as can be. Do you remember—how he says he wanted to get down on his knees and kiss the feet of the Negroes? That's the image in the book I think of most. It's powerful, man! I told my kid sister about it, and she said Agee must have been a pretty crazy white man to think like that. I asked her what she meant. She said no 'normal white man' thinks like that! She's eleven! She's pretty smart!"

The exact description of that particular scene offered by Agee goes like this: "They just kept looking at me. There was no more for them to say than for me. The least I could have done was to throw myself flat on my face and embrace and kiss their feet. That impulse took hold of me so powerfully, from my whole body, not by thought, that I caught myself from doing it exactly and as scarcely as you snatch yourself from jumping from a sheer height. . . ." He knew he would, indeed, be thought loony, or else a sinister confidence man, up to some mischief. Blacks, back then, had to put up with all sorts of white craziness in terror-struck or bitter and mocking silence. But what are we to make of the somewhat overwrought impulse of self-abasement that Agee comes so close to enacting? Is he exaggerating for dramatic purposes—a good storyteller's narrative impulse? Is he pushing us, morally and psychologically both— and educating us, as well: Here is what goes on down South, and here is how we ought feel? Might he be dismissed as the archetypal bleeding-heart liberal? Why did he bother that couple—who only wanted their privacy? And, of course, *that* question might be applied to the entire expedition: the vulnerability of the poor white folk interviewed and photographed and portrayed as so down-and-out, objects of pity for all the people rich enough to buy books.

Let Us Now Praise Famous Men is a great book precisely because it prompts such questions. What are the responsibilities of the various observers, investigators, writers who make their way into this or that community in hopes of discovering something, doing documentary work, finding "material" for an article, story, book? How much can one get to know about people if one spends a few days, a week or two, a month as a "guest" of theirs, a visitor with a deadline in mind? What are the assumptions a "we" (Agee and Evans, and countless other journalists, essayists, social scientists) bring to a "them"—and carry away, upon leaving? What matters are *not* discussed, even looked into, by those of us who do "field work"—and learn certain limits of conversation as we go from home to home? What topics does the observer-reporter censor deliberately or unconsciously?

The great strength of Agee's literary-journalistic writing was its provocativeness, its mixture of accurate, suggestive description, compassionate portraiture, skeptical cultural observation, and pungent social analysis, all rendered in a prose distinctively different from that of other documentary writers by virtue of its lyrical intensity. If there is any writing of Agee's that places him, tells us what, deep down, he believes, it is to be found in this paragraph, one that rescues the clichés of twentieth-century existentialist literature and philosophy, as they certainly must be rescued, from the banality of faddishness:

All that each person is, and experiences, and shall never experience, in body and in mind, all these things are differing expressions of himself and of one root, and are identical: and not one of these things nor one of these persons is ever quite to be duplicated, nor replaced, nor has it ever quite had precedent: but each is a new and incommunicably tender life, wounded in every breath, and almost as hardly killed as easily wounded: sustaining, for a while, without defense, the enormous assaults of the universe.

Those "assaults" did not spare his personal life. His second marriage, to Alma Mailman, did not last long, though it produced their son, Joel, now a fine writer in his own right.

He had a rough time in the late 1930s writing *Let Us Now Praise Famous Men*: He was constantly short of cash, and he wasn't at all sure how to present the families he'd met, nor how to present himself, as the one who saw and heard, who came and left, who writes and is read. The book was originally called *Three Tenant Farmers*. The decision, to change the title and use words from the *Apocrypha*—the book of Ecclesiasticus, chapter 44—was an extremely significant one. The reader is told, right off, that he or she must contend with a moral narrative, with a literary sensibility intent on irony, rather than with a more standard sociological study. Unsurprisingly, Agee's critical response to his own book was severely moral, if not moralistic. To Father Flye, in 1941, he wrote that "what you write of the book is good to hear to the point of shaming me—for it is a sinful book at least in all degrees of 'falling short of the mark' and I think in more corrupt ways as well."

◆　　◆　　◆

James Agee

PLANS FOR WORK: October 1937
(Submitted by James Agee with his application for a Guggenheim Fellowship)

I am working on, or am interested to try, or expect to return to, such projects as the following. I shall first list them, then briefly specify a little more about most of them.

An Alabama Record.
Letters.
A Story about homosexuality and football.
News Items.
Hung with their own rope.
A dictionary of key words.
Notes for color photography.
A revue.
Shakespeare.
A cabaret.
Newsreel. Theatre.
A new type of stage-screen show.
Anti-communist manifesto.
Three or four love stories.
A new type of sex book.
"Glamor" writing.
A study of the pathology of "laziness."
A new type of horror story.
Stories whose whole intention is the direct communication of
     the intensity of common experience.
"Musical" uses of "sensation" or "emotion."
Collections and analyses of faces; of news pictures.
Development of new forms of writing via the caption; Letters;
     pieces of overheard conversation.

A new form of "story": the true incident recorded as such and an analysis of it.

A new form of movie short roughly equivalent to the lyric poem.

Conjectures of how to get "art" back on a plane of organic human necessity, parallel to religious art or the art of primitive hunters.

A show about motherhood.

Pieces of writing whose rough parallel is the prophetic writings of the Bible.

Uses of the Dorothy Dix Method; the Voice of Experience: for immediacy, intensity, complexity of opinion.

The inanimate and non-human.

A new style and use of the imagination: the exact opposite of the Alabama record.

A true account of a jazz band.

An account and analysis of a cruise: "high"-class people.

Portraiture. Notes. The Triptych.

City Streets. Hotel Rooms. Cities.

A new kind of photographic show.

The slide lecture.

A new kind of music. Noninstrumental sound. Phonograph recordings. Radio.

Extension in writing; ramification in suspension; Schubert 2-cello Quintet.

Analyses of Hemingway, Faulkner, Wolfe, Auden, other writers.

Analyses of reviews of Kafka's *Trial*; various moving pictures.

Two forms of history of the movies.

Reanalyses of the nature and meaning of love.

Analyses of miscommunication; the corruption of idea.

Moving picture notes and scenarios.

An "autobiographical novel."

New forms of "poetry."

A notebook.

1938
Frenchtown, New Jersey

Dear Dwight [Macdonald]:

As you may have had wind of, Via and I are divorcing. I am here with Alma Mailman, whom you may but more likely do not know. I am at last, after some strained and chaotic months, getting to work on the tenant book. This is a good place to live for a while.

Alma Mailman Neuman

He wanted to work, and he wanted the quiet and peace of mind. He wanted to get out of the city. And we found a house in Frenchtown, New Jersey, and we set up housekeeping.

We had met at the Saunders house when I was about eighteen and he was about twenty-one. He was every young girl's dream of a poet. He was tall and gawky, had hair a little bit too long for those days; he was charming. He was very impressive, and then I had heard a lot about him beforehand. He was the genius of the Saunders family. He was the Harvard poet, and was about to be published. I'd heard all sorts of things about him, and I was very impressed. I was in awe of him. I remember going into a room when he was there and being tongue-tied, not wanting to be alone with him because I didn't know how to speak to him. I had probably heard too much about him.

We were in love. And it was something else, too. We met each other on other levels. First we met each other on music. And it wasn't just that we played together, or talked about music, or went to concerts. We *understood* something, that we met on music, which didn't need to be talked about. And we met on a religious basis which also you shouldn't use the word for. Also, he wanted to be with me; I wanted to be with him, and we moved to Frenchtown. We had a wood frame house with an upstairs, a downstairs, a back porch, and a big coal stove in the kitchen, and we were like two kids playing house. The first thing that happened was Walker Evans coming with a crate of Scotch whisky.

We were mostly alone. Walker and Helen used to come out. Helen didn't like to stay weekends because we had a mouse and as I said, I wasn't a very good housekeeper then, and she didn't like the idea of

Agee and Delmore Schwartz, Monk's Farm,
New Jersey, 1939. (Photos by Helen Levitt)

sharing a room with a mouse. And I don't think Walker approved of me, either. I guess no one approved of me then.

During the year that we were living there, we noticed that there were mice sharing the house with us. They lived between the walls of the house, and we left a large bag in the kitchen, which I used to put the garbage in at the end of the day. The mice used to make a little hole in the garbage and they fed themselves, and they lived very well there. Jim and I used to sit in the living room, and there was a rocker in there, and I remember if we sat very quietly the mice would come out, and they felt so at home that they would play in the living room. They really played; they played tag. Two of them would go in a large circle running after each other. There were six of them, and I think I could tell them apart. I didn't give them names, but I knew there were six.

Before we left Frenchtown, I knew that the people who were going to move in after us were going to set traps for "my mice," and I didn't want it to happen. Neither did Jim. So the night before we were supposed to move, I went to the five-and-ten and bought a live trap, and we put the trap in the kitchen. We were up until four in the morning waiting for the mice to come into the trap, and we had to help them into the trap because they were so fat. We caught five; one got away. I'd never do it again, but we took the mice with us to this summer place. I drove next to the truck driver and had my mice in my lap, and he looked down at me and thought I was crazy. And then he thought I was crazier because when we got to the house I took my little tray of mice, and I let them out into the house. I've never fed mice since, by the way—that was the last.

At any rate we lived. Mostly he worked at night. And during the day when he wasn't working we played; played tennis, piano. He played tennis the way he played piano—without any technique, but brilliant when it hit off. When he did get a drive over, no one could get it back. And he played piano that way, too. And we used to draw each other, too, and you get to know each other when you play music together, or draw each other.

It was a happy time. He'd finish writing and then read what he had written, and I thought that everything he wrote was marvelous. I had no sense of criticism. We'd feel good about it, and then about two or three

Alma Agee, James Agee, and Delmore Schwartz, Frenchtown,
New Jersey, 1939. (Photos by Helen Levitt)

in the morning, we'd get in the car and go for a ride. We'd go over the dirt roads around Frenchtown, and I'd get out on the running board, and he'd go as fast as he could. It was nice.

Jim was two people when I think now: the Harvard graduate and the tenant farmer, and I reacted to the farmer. I liked the big, clumsy, awkward, sensitive guy.

Jim got me a goat, a young goat, one of those charming, just-leaving-its-mother kind of goat. Very sweet. We kept it in the backyard, and it kept Jim from working because it would bleat. We were very fond of the goat so we kept it in the kitchen, thinking it would stop. It didn't. So we went to an auction to get another goat to keep it company, thinking that two goats would be quiet. We bought another goat, and then we had two goats, and they both naa'd all day long, and it was a disaster.

We took the goats to New York once, to Walker's place. I spent the afternoon picking grass to feed them, and we put both goats in the backseat of the car, drove them to New York, and took them up the elevator to Walker's place. There was a little roof and the goats spent the night there with their grass. And Walker was . . . he didn't like it. We took them home the next day.

Robert Fitzgerald

Frenchtown—a little frame house, weedy yard, goat in the yard, primitive kinds of furnishings. And the way that Jim dressed, and rather made a point of dressing, was not in business suits, but old blue work-shirts, always stained under the armpits where he had sweated. He was allying himself with the underprivileged, as we now, unfortunately, have gotten in the habit of calling them.

I'm sure that in changing his life he was moved by feelings that the Alabama experience had brought up in him. That is, I think, that bourgeois accoutrements and bourgeois routines were less acceptable to him, if anything, after he'd been to Alabama than they had been before, and that part of what was going on was that he was deliberately setting his face against the sort of quiet life that I've described—him living with

Agee at Monk's Farm, New Jersey, 1939.
(Photos by Helen Levitt)

Via in the little apartment on Perry Street and doing the job for *Fortune*. After that trip to Alabama that became much less possible for him. In fact, it became possible again, really, only toward the end of the war; only in the mid-forties, I think, did he again feel that kind of thing was okay. After all, it was an extreme into which he fell: if you decide that even being clean—you know, simple physical cleanliness, washing—is a sinful alliance of yourself with bourgeois values. He got over that in time.

Alma Mailman Newman

Jim was working at *Time*, and Henry R. Luce heard that Jim didn't look the way other people looked when they came to work. Everyone else wore neat suits and had their hair cut in crew cuts in the way people dressed in those days. Jim rarely went to the barber's, and he didn't wear a tie, and he was sloppy. Jim heard that Henry Luce didn't like the way he dressed. I think he got a memo to "watch it." So Jim went out and bought himself one of those little roll-brimmed hats that they sell in Times Square; strange people would wear them. A green feather was in it. He wore that up the elevator—this little narrow-brimmed hat with the green feather in it—he wore it the next day up the elevator, and down, with all these primly dressed people on it. He loved that hat. He wore it for years.

James Agee

Summer, 1939
Monks Farm, New Jersey

Dear Robert [Fitzgerald],

Is your work of a sort that you could do stretches of it out of town? Because if so, nothing would make us happier than that you do it here. Good schedules are kept and there is plenty of room for privacy and silence for work. . . . Do think of it seriously, for it would be entirely possible to us, and I think would for all of us be a good way to live.

Except for endless and awful delays in mechanical finishing of the book, living is just now about perfectly good. I wish all elements of such a situation could hold (not stand still, but another kind of hold), and that time ran slower.

Robert Fitzgerald

At parties sometimes in those days Jim would perform a parody of the Stokowski version of Bach's "Toccata and Fugue, in D Minor." He made himself into a one-man orchestra to parody the fruity effects that the orchestration had imposed on the pure work of the great musician that Bach was. And yet the reason for parodying was not just to have fun with your friends, but to express something held in common by you and your friends, which was indignation and revulsion over the cheapening, commercialization, and vulgarization of pure honest works of art, that was by us in those days identified with the deterioration of latter-day capitalism. That's something very important in the thinking of Agee: that what he honored and felt we ought to honor was what was honest and authentic and conscientious and pure in the making of works of music, works of theater, works of writing, or works of cinema, and that everything that was phony—that was a great word with him—was to be avoided and named for what it was.

I think that more than any man I have ever known, more, I would say, than any other man who engaged in writing in English in my lifetime, he insisted upon respect for the real, for a reality conceived not as one belonging to a school of realists, but as a religious man would feel toward the real, confronting what he regarded as the created world, a world created from moment to moment by a power beyond conception. To respect this in all its details, ambiguities, peculiarities, and finenesses was his aim. This, above all, was what he loved, and truth in this sense was his desire. To be true to things as they were. Of course, the epitome of the whole effort was the terrible exertion to do this with the lives of the people in Alabama. That is what I call the centerpiece of his life and his work.

Walker Evans

Agee was really a much more powerful, intense, and interesting man than you would expect to work with, and as such presented enormous difficulties, too. He required a great deal of understanding and forebearance and was very hard to handle because he had violent tendencies when frustrated, and there was a lot of frustration in that work. He used to get so angry at not being able to go ahead and do what he wanted to do, and his rage was paralyzing to him and to everyone around him. I don't see how he kept enough control of himself to do such controlled work. He didn't look like a man disciplined enough to do what he did do. So there was a surprising sort of confusion between Agee's appearance as I saw it and his accomplishment, which is on record as being tremendous.

Dwight Macdonald

Agee and Walker had a very close relationship, a friendship, and more than a friendship, I think. I think that they really needed each other. I think they were both geniuses, you know, whatever that word means; they were both men of supreme, original talent. I think they complemented each other, and it's much to the credit of both of them that they recognized this, because they couldn't be more different in style, and so on.

If you notice on the title page, this [*Famous Men*] is not by James Agee; it's by James Agee *and* Walker Evans. He's on the title page; he's not just an illustrator. I think he had quite a lot to do with the editing of the book, too. He's one of the few people that Agee would ever ask advice of. And that may be one reason the book is what it is. I mean that as a friend he certainly read the manuscript before it was published, and I think that he probably made some suggestions that Agee would take. Agee wouldn't take any suggestions from any editor at all. No, there was no editing otherwise. You don't edit Agee, no.

One of the reasons he was so good in *Let Us Now Praise Famous Men* is that he didn't have any sense of limits or bounds. Therefore, he would go on for five pages describing the intricate grains of wood in a wall, or something like that. It's like *Ulysses*. It's not as great a book as *Ulysses*, but it's comparable—all kinds of styles and all kinds of subject matter. He tried everything; he never gave up. He was terribly ambitious that way.

But of course, on the other hand, he was completely without any self-protection. He didn't have any of that carapace, that crablike armor that protects us from the radiations of the outside world. He didn't have that at all; he was open to everything. Every day I'm sure for him was a new beginning.

There's more of Agee in that book than anything else he did. Some people think too much of Agee. But I think that's a good fault, really. He was big enough, had a big enough personality.

Father Flye

In the early summer of '39, I came up to New York just to see him. He had separated from Via. I wasn't with him when that was going on. Then he married Alma, and when I came up they were just on the point of going out to a place near Flemington, New Jersey, to a place that was out in a field, half a mile from the nearest house, I guess. The house had been built in 1700 and something, I don't know whether it would have been very habitable in the winter, but it was all right in the summer. A well out in the field, and a toilet out there, and kerosene lamps, and quite primitive, which he loved. He was just finishing the last touches of *Let Us Now Praise Famous Men*. I gave him all the time that he needed to work on that until he finished it.

After several days Jim said, "Well it's done, we'll take the manuscript in to Harpers." So we got in the car, and we started in with the manuscript to be delivered, and partway in he said, "I've just had an idea that I could rewrite a whole section of that book." And we took it back. And that was in '39, and it was about two years later that it got published. He transferred publishers. That was Harpers and he transferred over to Houghton Mifflin.

James Agee

Dear Father Flye,

My writing is in bad shape. The past five weeks have been completely sterile. My trouble is that such a subject cannot be seriously looked at without intensifying itself toward a center which is beyond what I or anyone else is capable of writing of—the whole problem and nature of existence. Well, there's no use trying to talk about it; if I could make it what it ought to be made, I would not be human.

FROM Let Us Now Praise Famous Men

Here at a center is a creature: it would be our business to show how through every instant of every day of every year of his existence alive he is from all sides streamed inward upon, bombarded, pierced, destroyed by that enormous sleeting of all objects forms and ghosts how great how small no matter. . . .

{We} try at least to suggest also his incomparable tenderness to experience, his malleability, the almost unimaginable nakedness . . . the size, the pity, the abomination of the crimes he is to sustain, against the incredible sweetness, strength, and beauty of what he might be and is cheated of. . . .

For one who sets himself to look at all earnestly . . . into the living eyes of a human life: what is it he there beholds that so freezes and abashes his ambitious heart? What is it, profound behind the outward windows . . . drawn tightly back at bay against the backward wall and blackness of its prison cave, so that the eyes alone shine of their own angry glory, but the eyes of a trapped wild animal, or of a furious angel nailed to the ground by his wings, or however else one may faintly designate the human "soul," that which is angry, that which is wild, that which is untameable, that which is healthful and holy.

*Agee entering farmhouse where he and Alma lived in Monk's
farm, New Jersey, 1939. (Photo by Helen Levitt)*

Alma Mailman Neuman

He was gentle unless he was drinking; then he could get violent. His violence was never against people; it was against situations or against himself. He might hit his head against a stone building after leaving a party or a situation which would upset him; people's pain used to upset him. I remember Jim's dissolving into tears, crying over someone he didn't know—a bank teller, just a small person spending his life doing a job. He was thinking of him; thought of his whole life and the pain of it and the loss of it, I guess, and he just cried. He was a lovable, gentle, great guy. His lovableness, I think, was impossible for anyone to resist.

Shortly before I went to Mexico, I went to the Time-Life Building one night. Jim had a deadline to meet and it was very late. We quarreled, and I insisted I wanted to go, but he wanted me to stay. He threatened me. He said he was going to jump out of the window. It was on the twentieth floor. There was a glass ledge, and he went over and put one long leg over the glass ledge and looked back at me with this defiant look on his face. I just looked at him and left—walked down to the elevator. And as I got to the elevator I thought, Oh my God, I've made him do it, and I ran back into the room. This was very late at night, and no one else was working. I ran into the room and the window was open and there was no Jim. The room was empty. I ran over to the window, frightened, really frightened, and I looked down. I don't know what I expected to find. I saw nothing, except what you see when you look out the twentieth floor from a window, and turned around and there was Jim behind the door, looking a little sheepish. I think I left about two weeks later.

When I left for Mexico it was after a dreadful year. It was after Joel was born, and Joel's birth meant a change in Jim's and my life. Jim's way of living and working continued. He slept as long as he felt like, stayed up talking during the night, worked. And I, almost overnight, became a mother and responsible for a baby, and I almost didn't see him anymore. And I became different—I had a baby. I don't think Jim changed; he still loved me, but I was different.

Then there was the situation which happened, which came with

Mia, and this conflict went on. I guess maybe he wanted both, I don't know. I know that I couldn't take the situation and the baby. And then after about a year of this, which involved two or three attempts on my part to run and being pulled back, attempts at suicide of Jim's, but not serious ones I don't think, just histrionic displays. And then Helen Levitt and I went to Mexico.

It was thought at that time, or spoken of, that I would be away for three months, and then come back and everything would be fine. I think inside myself I knew I didn't want to come back. I went to Mexico and I didn't come back. I met my second husband there with whom Jim became friends later.

It wasn't the last time I saw Jim, but I remember we went on the Grace Lines, and I remember Jim coming to say good-bye, and it was a cold April day, and his coat open and tears running down his face. It's a sweet and painful memory of him.

James Agee

December 1940

Dear Robert [Fitzgerald],

. . . Everyone I see, myself included, is at a low grinding ebb of quiet desperation. Nothing, in most cases, *out of the ordinary*, just the general average Thoreau was telling about, plus the dead ends of one of the most evil years in history, plus each individual's little specialty act. . . . It isn't as bad as I've perhaps suggested, except by contrast with health and free action—is, in fact, just the average experience of people living as people shouldn't, doing what people shouldn't, where people shouldn't, and little or nothing of what people should. Journalists, hacks, husbands, wives, sisters, neurotics, self-harmed artists, and such. Average New York fall.

I must learn my ways in an exceedingly quiet marriage (which can be wonderful I've found out, but is basically not at all my style or apparent "nature") or break from marriage and all close liaisons altogether and learn how to live alone and keep love at a bearable distance.

These are oddly juvenile things to be beginning to learn at my age. What really baffles me is that, knowing them quite well since I was fifteen, I've done such thorough jobs in the opposite direction.

My business now and evidently for quite a while to come is evidently to sit as tight and careful as I can, taking care above all to do no further harm to others or myself or my, by now, virtually destroyed needs or hopes. . . . I haven't been very intelligent—to say nothing of "good"—. . . On the whole though, it's time I had a good hard dose of bad going. . . . Meanwhile though, I find I'm so dull I bore myself sick. A broken spirit and a contrite heart have their drawbacks: worst of all, if at the same time the spirit is unbroken and ferocious and the heart contrite only in the sense of deep grief over pain and loss. . . .

The book is supposed to be published in January or February, no proofs yet. I now thoroughly regret using the subtitle *Let Us Now Praise Famous Men* as I should have never forgotten I would. I am rather curious to look at it, finished and in print—possibly also to read it in that form—but I have an idea I'll be unable to stand to. If so, it might be a healthy self-scorching to force myself to: but that is probably my New England Chapel-crank blood.

Mainly, though, I want to be through with it and to get to work again as soon as I can. I am thirty-one now, and I can conceivably forgive myself the last ten years only by a devotion to work in the next ten which I suspect I will be incapable of. I am much too vulnerable to human relationship, particularly sexual or in any case heterosexual, and much too deeply wrought on by them, and in turn much too dependent in my work upon "feeling" as against "intellect." In short I'm easily upset and when upset incapable of decent work; incapable of it also when I'm not upset enough.

Ellie Mae Burroughs

I don't guess it's been over ten years ago that I seen the book, if it's been that long. My daughter got one of 'em; I don't know where in the world she got it, but she got it and told me she had it, and she wanted me to look at it and give it to me. And I took it home and I read it plumb through. And when I read it plumb through I give it back to her and I said, "Well everything in there's true." What they wrote in there was true.

And now, since then now, they've had other books to come out with different pictures in 'em of my husband. My son over there, he's got one of 'em now, and says he likes it because Floyd was called "famous," you know. He's got one of his pictures over there on the wall now, and he says he's glad his daddy was counted in the bunch. But now, my oldest boy, he just don't go for it. He said that my daddy wasn't half-dressed, and he just thinks they ought not to've done it. But I don't care, 'cause it was true. They even talked about suing them when that book first came out, some of the kids did. And that's when I told 'em. I said, well I don't know what you're going to sue them for, 'cause I wouldn't want to hurt 'em if I could, because they was too good to me.

Father Flye

Think of when it came out. We were just getting into the Second World War, and who wanted to read about Alabama tenant farmers when the world was in flames? It came out at one of the worst times that could have been. I don't know how popular it would have been in any case. I don't suppose it would have sold a great many, perhaps, but it would have had more influence than it had if it had come in a favorable time.

David McDowell

According to Jim Agee, there were only about three reviews that seemed to have the vaguest ideas of what he was trying to do. The best was Trilling's. There was another review in the *Memphis Commercial Appeal* by a brilliant young southern writer, long dead now, I'm afraid, named George Marion O'Donnell. It puzzled almost everybody, and that was part of the thing he was trying to do. He was trying to approach various kinds of angles and deliberately trying to provoke the reader, either from far left or the right or what have you—not the whole book, but there are areas in it right from the beginning where he was trying to needle the reader. And, the New York scene—literary scene—when the book came out in 1941 was, I won't say dominated, but largely influenced by the far left, either Trotskyite or communist, or ultra-ultra-liberal. And a good many of them were as much put off by it as Senator Bilbo from Mississippi would have been.

He was plowing new ground, and he was helped enormously in this by his tremendous interest in and knowledge of films and photographs, which went back to the time when he was in his teens. There was a lot of documentary work started in the thirties, but Jim just raised it up to a completely different level.

It sold about eight hundred copies of the approximately fifteen hundred copies printed by Houghton Mifflin. And it began to get, over a period of years, a sort of word-of-mouth following among a small group of people. But it was not reprinted until I forced the issue after the publication of *A Death in the Family*, and after he won the Pulitzer Prize. When he died not a single thing of his was in print anywhere, except in anthologies. *Permit Me Voyage* was out of print; *The Morning Watch* was out of print; *Let Us Now Praise Famous Men* was out of print. There were no collections of his scripts or of his film criticism and, of course, *A Death in the Family* had not been published. So, one of my functions as his friend and editor, and after his death, as his trustee, was to get him back into print. And now, everything he ever wrote, including the shorter prose and the poetry and the film criticism, the film scripts and everything else is in print, both in hardback and paperback, both in this country and in England.

Part 3

Man's Fate

has been forever shaped between the hands of reason and spirit, now in collaboration, again in conflict. Now reason and spirit meet on final ground. If either or anything is to survive, they must find a way to create an indissoluable partnership.

—Time, August 20, 1945

About the time *Let Us Now Praise Famous Men* was published, Agee began doing film reviews for *Time*. A year later he also began writing a column on films for *The Nation*. Even in his response to movies, the moral self-examination continued. One finds a ceaseless and familiar preoccupation with what is right and what is wrong. Nor did Agee confine himself to aesthetic distinctions—what is right or wrong with respect to camera technique, the use of sound, and so on. A review, for instance, of the war movie *Guadalcanal Diary* that appeared in *The Nation* on November 13, 1943, describes the film as "unusually serious, simple, and honest, as far as it goes." But Agee is quick to add, "It would be a shame and worse if those who made or will see it got the idea that it is a remotely adequate image of the first months on that island."

All through World War II, when American moviegoers were understandably glad to see the Japanese finally hard-pressed in the Pacific (*Guadalcanal Diary*), or to see the Germans begin to get their due (*Passage to Marseilles*), Agee was insistent upon the same frustrating, demanding, enraging complexity he'd offered in his Alabama book. On March 11, 1944, when this country was in its deepest engagement with both Hitler and the Japanese, Agee reviewed two films for *The Nation* in this manner:

> The Purple Heart *is Darryl Zanuck beating his Hollywood rivals to the draw with a Japanese atrocity picture. It is a fictional account, much more controlled than it might have been, of the trial and torture of eight American fliers who were captured after the Doolittle raid. Under Lewis Milestone's direction, his best in years, it is unusually edged, well-organized, and solidly acted. But I feel extremely queasy watching fiction—especially persuasive fiction—which pretends to clarify facts that are not clear, and may never become so. Conditioned by such amphibious and ambiguous semi-information, we are still more likely than otherwise to do things to defeated enemies which, both morally and materially, will finally damage us more deeply even than them.*
>
> *I feel an even sharper objection to the moment, in* Passage to Marseille, *when Humphrey Bogart, on a ship representing France, slaughters the surviving helpless crew of a wrecked plane which represents conquered Germany. Victor Francen is shocked, to be sure; but Bogart is the star, from whom the majority will accordingly accept advice on what to do with Germany. Aside from this scene the picture is regulation Nordhoff and Hall, Warner Brothers, Michael Curtiz fustian about Devil's Island, French fascists, and French patriots—fair-to-dull melodramatic entertainment, needled with political consciousness.*

A singular voice for that time, for any time, perhaps. A film critic with a marvelously crisp writing style (in contrast to the labored, con-

trived, taxing high Anglican prose of *Let Us Now Praise Famous Men*!).
Agee had a continuing interest in championing forgotten or overlooked
films. His list of "underdogs" was seemingly limitless; his compassion
was broad and deep, if sometimes startling, even (arguably) perverse.
His timing as a critic was often dramatic: the unfriendly thrust at FDR
in 1936 (discussed earlier), when the president was at the height of his
popularity for reasons, one assumes, with which Agee would sym-
pathize; a plea on behalf of postwar Japan and Germany, when American
men were still dying day after day in the fighting.

His reviews tended to be fairly short, and usually gave a quick
summary of the plot, a pointed judgment of a given director's success or
failure, an analysis of one or another movie star's abilities or pitiable
inadequacies. Occasionally, a review became quite personal. In January
1944 Agee started a commentary on *The Song of Bernadette* with this frank
statement:

> *Since nothing is more repugnant to me than the pseudoreligious, I went to*
> The Song of Bernadette *gritting my teeth against my advance loath-*
> *ing. But since, also, many of the deepest resonances of my childhood are*
> *Catholic; and since I intensely suspect and fear the implacable pieties of*
> *those who deny the rationally inexplicable even when they are being*
> *beaten over the head with it; and since, accordingly, I feel a triumphant*
> *pride in the work or mere existence of true artists and of the truly*
> *experienced in religion, I was unexpectedly and greatly moved by a great*
> *many things in the film. I owe this somewhat indecently subjective preface*
> *because I doubt that the film can be strongly recommended to anyone*
> *whose mind and emotions lack some similar shape. I can add only that*
> *the picture is unusually well made—within limits.*

Of course, those "limits" were immediately set down—the left
hand taking away what the right one had offered: "The limits are those of
middle-class twentieth-century genteelism, a fungus which soon all but
chokes the life out of any hope from Hollywood and which threatens any
vivid appetite in Hollywood's audience." It is interesting to compare the
Time review Agee did on the same film: "*The Song of Bernadette* lacks the

razor-edged realism, the urgent poetry, the freshet-like creative vitality of great cinema or great religious vision," he announces. He then praises the film as, nevertheless, "reverent, spiritually forthright, dignified." He dwells on Jennifer Jones as a new and promising star, rather than on the bourgeoisie and its various fungal problems.

The Song of Bernadette had touched perhaps the biggest chord in Agee's life. In *Let Us Now Praise Famous Men* he had mentioned, at one point, his own childhood, when "in the innocence of faith" he had served "at the altar at earliest lonely Mass." Even before he'd gone to Alabama, he'd begun work, as mentioned, on what would end up being the short novel (or long short story) *The Morning Watch*. It was published in 1951 by Houghton Mifflin, and its subject was faith versus doubt, ascetic purity and dedication to God's inscrutable will versus the sensuous, inviting pleasures of the equally inscrutable, here-and-now world of nature. There is scant effort to conceal the autobiographical elements, picked up where he left off in *A Death in the Family*. Rufus has become "Richard." He is twelve and his father has died. He is on the brink of adolescence, and his mother has enrolled him at an Episcopal boarding school in Tennessee because she wants him to be in the company of good, strong religious men and boys of his own age.

The title of the story comes from the 130th Psalm: "Thy soul fleeth unto the Lord before the morning watch." It takes place during the late part of Easter week, starting with the night before Good Friday, that most solemn day of the Christian calendar. The boy, Richard, wants to stay awake through the night and be part of his school's prayerful acknowledgment of Christ's awe-ful (and awesome) suffering. He fails, by falling asleep, is awakened, and does his duty at the first watch, then decides to stay through the second, though he has been told he ought to go to bed. When the second watch is over, Richard joins two others in a swimming expedition. They return, finally, to school: a night over, Good Friday in full sway, another day of their lives before them.

The story is a somewhat strained attempt to approach the inevitable angelical-bestial polarity that becomes especially intense during the years of emerging adulthood. Richard is zealously devout yet plagued by his own humanity. He recognizes in himself idle curiosity, boastfulness, envy, and greed, the thrill of the body's response to the outer and inner world.

The narrator, intent on giving us such conflict thoroughly nuanced and subtle, is unmistakably James Agee: "In hidden vainglory he had vowed that he would stay awake straight through the night, for he had wondered, and not without scorn, how they, grown men, could give way to sleep on this night of all the nights in their life, leaving Him without one friend in His worst hour." How many novelists who went to Exeter and Harvard and lived in Greenwich Village and drank lots and lots of bourbon and reviewed movies for *The Nation* and smoked packs of cigarettes and had a keen appreciation of jazz would start a story with those words: "In hidden vainglory"? They are words that tell a lot about Agee—about his war with his own pride as it became connected to twentieth-century secular forms of expression. One can read Agee and see him as a Christian psychologist in the tradition of Kierkegaard and Pascal—always at watch over his mind's twin desires, to find a God he can believe in and to find himself so that his belief can live. And the struggle was tied to authority, as he makes clear in Richard's shrewd appraisal of those Episcopal monk teachers. As a quick-witted youth Agee had spotted in others, no matter their high position or claim to virtue, that eternal gap between pronouncement and performance—between abstract insistence and concrete realization. All through his life he had a scent for hypocrisy, for high-minded postures which, upon close examination, turn out to be artfully contrived concealments. The Richard who questioned adults became the Jim who mocked secular priests, their magazines, their slogans, their whole manner of living; the Jim who, needless to say, gave himself the hardest look of all.

By the middle 1940s Agee was doing special feature stories for *Time*—the cover story, for instance, on the use by this country of the atomic bomb in August 1945. In 1946 he married Mia Fritsch, a union that, in the less than ten years left to Agee, would result in two daughters and one son. In 1948 he left *Time* and made his last decisive shift, toward film—not as a reviewer, but as a scriptwriter. That year he wrote two film scripts, both for Stephen Crane stories, *The Blue Hotel* and *The Bride Comes to Yellow Sky*. He wrote articles for *Life* magazine in 1949 and 1950 on Hollywood and on silent film comedians, and he also wrote a piece on the director John Huston. In late 1950 he was working in Hollywood himself with Huston, writing a script for a movie based on C. S. Forester's novel *The African Queen*.

His life there was pure Agee—long, intense conversation, plenty of drinking and smoking, intense work, much of it at night, and little sleep. He had planned to be in California through a major part of the winter of 1950–51. But in early 1951 a heart attack struck. Though he was only forty-one, this was the beginning of the end. Angina plagued him during the remaining four years of his life.

In those years, despite his cardiac problems, he was productive. He wrote scripts for a life of Lincoln, for a movie to be based on Gauguin's diaries, and for the film *Night of the Hunter*. His letters to Father Flye reveal a man both hopeful and despondent; a man aware that he was in medical trouble, yet hoping against hope that things would work out favorably; a man struggling hard against powerfully addictive bad habits, smoking especially; and not least, a lion of a man, now struggling against the terrible toll exacted by a deadly disease. Bravely, he pushed on; his mind kept its usual feverish pace, and his interests, his preferences, as always, spoke eloquently of his character.

He liked very much, for instance, Charles Chaplin—saw in his work a triumphant, searching social and political criticism, all worked into a brilliant artist's performance. Agee the passionate moralist, angry at injustice and anxious to change the world, saw in Chaplin a fellow artist with similar interests and loyalties. There was, too, a homelessness to Chaplin's life that touched Agee deeply; both men had little use for the territorial imperatives to which many of us bow uncritically: my country, right or wrong. Agee was, moreover, a gifted mimic, a man with a wonderful sense of humor, and of course, a dedicated film critic to whom satire was especially appealing.

His interest in Lincoln and Gauguin deserves notice. He was a Lincolnesque figure himself, tall and gangly and rough-hewn, with rumpled dark hair and eyes both piercing and brooding. He came from the same region as Lincoln—the Tennessee and Kentucky precincts of

Appalachia's yeoman country. He resembled Lincoln intellectually—a strong kinship with the humble, the outcast, and a dislike for the affectations and depredations carried on by the well-to-do and influential. Both men were ambitious and not prepared to yield in the face of any kind of snobbish power. Lincoln was a realist, and knew how to hold his own, and then some; Agee was no fool about how things worked—in the world of magazines and newspapers, in the world of Hollywood, or in the realm of politics. There was, finally, a noble sadness to Lincoln, a loneliness, which Agee must have recognized. Often he wrote to Father Flye, in letter after letter, about his own isolation and unhappiness.

The life of Paul Gauguin must have resonated in other ways for Agee—the stubborn insistence to somehow be an honorable and worthwhile artist, no matter the personal cost. Gauguin's vision was brilliantly original and eccentric. He dared give up everything for that vision. He was another homeless one—a wanderer, a dreamer who demanded that his dreams be accepted on their own terms. There was an explicit arrogance to Gauguin; in Agee one saw humility holding in check a similar "pride," as he himself knew and said in his letters, and as he successfully evoked in his two novels. Neither of these two men could be described as personally happy and contented. Both were restless, sharply imaginative, intensely scrutinizing, disturbingly meditative artists.

The great Gauguin triptych done in 1898, titled *Where Do We Come From? What Are We? Where Are We Going?*, was completed just before the artist made a dramatic suicide attempt. The painting, lodged in Boston's Museum of Fine Arts, is a masterpiece of symbolic and narrative presentation—a testimonial offering by an artist both dying and full of aesthetic and spiritual vitality. Gauguin, like Agee, was constantly asking questions about this life we live—offering us humanity in the most basic way one can, through an exploration of our distinctive capacity for awareness. I do not mean to equate in any definitive, psychological manner those two turbulent artists. I merely see connections in their gifted struggle, their brooding philosophical preoccupations, their refusal to take for granted the ordinary, conventional ways of looking at the world, their tenacious determination to find a point of view that does justice to certain ideals, no matter the personal cost.

Moreover, Gauguin knew only too well how hard it is to do justice to the demands of an inner vision so that it can be released and shared with others. When a painter resorts to words, as he did, something terribly important, even desperately pressing, is likely at stake. Gauguin remarked upon "the futility of vain words," an idea given pictorial representation in the triptych: a white bird sits with a lizard in its claws, the lizard symbolizing a destructive or greedy side of human life; the animal in us, which is a given. Such hopelessness with respect to our prospects as the one creature driven by the effort of making some sense of things—these feelings of discouragement were repeatedly evident in Agee as he tried hard to perform the magic of the writer. So often he judged himself to have missed the mark. He turned to photographs, as he tells us in *Let Us Now Praise Famous Men*, because, like Gauguin, he knew that "futility," which the thought of "vain words" can sometimes inspire in an earnest, sensitive writer. Still, he wrote, even as Gauguin, for all his despondency, kept asking certain questions and kept trying to answer them with his brushes and paints.

In the last months of his life Agee consciously stared death in the face, as Gauguin did in Tahiti. Any episode of pain, he well knew, could be the heralding prologue of another coronary occlusion. Under such circumstances he tried hard to conserve his limited energy; and he worked away on his novel *A Death in the Family*, which would be published posthumously.

This novel is an ambitious one, indeed: an effort to tell a story through the eyes of a young boy who learned of his father's death in an automobile accident, and who then tried to understand not only death itself, but the various responses to death he sees in his family—the turmoil in his mother, his grandparents, his aunt and uncle. Agee had always sought the purity (as he, and his Christian sensibility, saw it) of a child's vision; in this novel he tries to render that vision whole—a searching evocation of what children make of this world's puzzles, its loony moments and its rather ordinary but touching, even sometimes quite stirring, moments. It is a substantial feat—to sustain a story through the workings of a child's mind—and Agee brings to the effort all his lyrical powers in no way diminished by his weakened heart.

That heart, so big and tender in its response to this world, finally stopped working on May 16, 1955. Agee was in a taxi in midtown New

York on his way to a doctor's appointment. He felt the attack coming on, asked the driver to take him to the hospital. He was dead on arrival. He was buried on his farm in Hillsdale, New York. The service was held at St. Luke's in New York City; Father Flye presided. Father Flye was in Omaha, Nebraska, at the time of Agee's death. When Flye got to New York he found on the mantel in Agee's living room a letter waiting to be mailed to him from Agee. It is printed in the published collection of letters from Agee to Flye. His friends and family gathered in sad and loving tribute to an utterly unique and extraordinary human being. A telegram from one well-known friend said "I loved him," and no doubt to this day, even among those of us who are from the generations that have followed his, the same words come readily to mind.

♦   ♦   ♦

Father Flye

Mia and her mother and two brothers had come to this country from Austria, their native land. They were not Jews but they were not Nazis. They came during the Hitler regime, when the clouds were thickening. Mia had never been married. She was a researcher on *Fortune*, which is where they met. There was perhaps one period that he regretted that he couldn't be married to both Alma and Mia. But that isn't done somehow in this country. So he and Alma broke up, and he married Mia and they had three children. That was a good marriage. They played duets together and that sort of thing. They had a house on King Street, on the lower edge of the Village.

Mia Fritsch Agee

He always wrote. I mean he always, always wrote. Jim never took a day off, basically. If we did something in the evening, then he would come home, sit down, and start writing. I mean he'd never have a full twenty-four hours without doing some writing. Never. If he took a vacation, it was in order to write. It meant being free of having to work for *Time* or having to work for whomever. A vacation was time for him to do his own writing.

Robert Fitzgerald

I think Jim Agee was, most clearly of anyone I've ever known, a born writer. Haven't I mentioned that he had, in later years, a callus on the middle finger of his hand as big as a boil, from gripping the pencil for so many years. I've never seen anyone who had that stigmata that he had.

And, in a sense, I think it always came easy for him, if he could bring himself to it. The difficulty always was to clear away the distractions that he liked: music, movies, company, and so on, and then square

James and Mia Agee in New York City. (Photo by Helen Levitt)

James Agee at Bleecker Street apartment, New York City, date unknown. (Photo by Helen Levitt)

James and Mia Agee in New York City.
(Photo by Helen Levitt)

away to do the writing. Once he was at it, once he had his mind on it, I think it came very easily to him, and he wrote copiously. He wrote a great deal.

I remember in fact one great scene at *Time*. His office was always a huge chaos of old newspapers, books, letters, unopened correspondence, and so on. And when he came to work he would literally burrow a kind of clearing in this tremendous mess on the desk, clear himself, say, four square feet of space. Then the yellow paper, a bunch of it, would be put down, and the pencils, the sharpened pencils. Then one had the impression of enormous force being concentrated literally like a beam of light on this small space that he had cleared away. And the world otherwise vanished, because it was all concentrated there—his mind, his whole being, his physical being concentrated on what he was writing. So that one had the feeling that there was a real solid shaft of intellectual light falling from this rather frowning brow down on the paper in front of him. A very impressive exhibition.

Time was, of course, a news machine. But the books division was much less like that. There, one could come in on Thursday, as we all did, and have what we called a conference about the books. The secretary would have typed up a list of books to be published in the given week. We'd go through the list, and see what sounded interesting or promising, and divide the books. And you could take them then—you could take them home, or take them to read on a subway, or in the park, or wherever you liked. When you wanted to use your typewriter in your office, there it was. If you liked you could come in at two A.M. and write from two A.M. to six A.M. and then go home and go to bed, so long as the reviews were done on the deadline day. So it was rather irregular, and it was not so office bound as the newswriters were. It was, of all possible jobs that Jim could've had at *Time*, the most possible.

Film reviews were, of course, much the same. I mean, he would go to the previews of the films, come into the office and write the reviews, and that was that. Well, he loved it—he really did. That was, in a way, another decisive moment in Jim's life. I think it was at the end of that year or so when he and I did books together. I don't know who had been doing cinema, but something happened and they handed it to Jim. That began the whole new cinema period.

Agee on fire escape of Bleecker Street apartment, New York City, c. 1945. (Photo by Helen Levitt)

After a while, since he was seeing the movies, since he had a lot more to say about them than he could possibly say in two or three columns of *Time*, the *Nation* gave him a job, or allowed him every other week a page or so, in which he could say what he wanted to say about the movies. And this led in time to going to Hollywood and all the rest of it. This was a little watershed in his life.

Dwight Macdonald

I think as a critic he suffered from the fact that he really wanted to be a creator. His criticism, I think, is extremely good. It's good because he has a broad cultural background, he's got great style, he can say things in two sentences, he has intelligence, wit, and precision; and also he really does have a sense of values and he doesn't give them up. But as a person who wanted to be a creator, he kept seeing in movies all kinds of things that really weren't there. You see, I'm a critic; I'm a noncreative critic, and I always have been. I never wanted to write any fiction or poetry after I got out of Yale. I would tend to see a movie or any work of art as a whole. Agee used to find some beauties in these films, some of which I don't think were there at all, but if he had been making them, they would have been.

He would say, "Oh, you must see this." And I'd say, "Well, come on. Listen, that's just another one of those machine-made things." He'd say, "But didn't you notice the beginning of the fourth reel—that great scene where he picks up his toothbrush?" or something like that. And I'd say, "Well, I didn't really."

He took the appearance for the deed. I think the main trouble with his criticism is that it often tends to be much too uncritical. For instance, I think his overestimation of Chaplin's film *Monsieur Verdoux* came because he could see so clearly what Chaplin was trying to do, which was a very admirable thing—make fun of the whole bourgeois system, and so on. But what he had to talk away was the fact that Chaplin in that film fails quite badly in doing it. To Agee, you see, this wouldn't be so visible. But he's still probably our best, certainly one of our best, film critics here. That's not saying very much, by the

(Photos by Helen Levitt)

(*Photo by Helen Levitt*)

way. I mean film criticism has never been very good, anywhere; I don't know why.

He did love the cinema, but the great tragedy was that he couldn't—didn't—make his own things. His scripts are very good—*The Bridge Comes to Yellow Sky* and *The African Queen*—and he really would have made an extraordinary director, I think. He died too soon, you see. By the time he'd died, it wasn't so uncommon. All kinds of people were making movies, you know, rather cheaply in fact. He could've, in the next five years, easily done something. But he didn't. He died—and he died because he wouldn't restrain himself.

Father Flye

Yes, this was in August, and I was taking summer duty at St. Luke's Chapel, and early one evening Jim Agee came over and said at once, "Have you heard any news today?" And I said, "No, I haven't. I didn't get a paper, and I haven't had the radio on today, so I haven't." And he said, "You'd better get a good, stiff drink. They have discovered the secret of atomic power and have made a bomb of tremendously destructive power and have dropped it on Japan." And he was deeply moved. He wrote, by the way, the cover story for *Time* on the atomic bomb. He was much impressed by putting this enormous amount of destructive power into the hands of human beings. And so was I.

James Agee

[From the *Time* magazine cover story of August 20, 1945]

The greatest and most terrible of wars ended this week in the echoes of an enormous event. The rational mind had put into the hands of common man the fire and force of the sun itself. When the bomb split open the universe, and revealed the prospect of the infinitely extraordinary, it also revealed the oldest, simplest, commonest, most neglected and most important of facts—that each man is eternally and, above all else, responsible for his own soul.

James and Mia Agee playing the piano,
date unknown. (Photos by Helen Levitt)

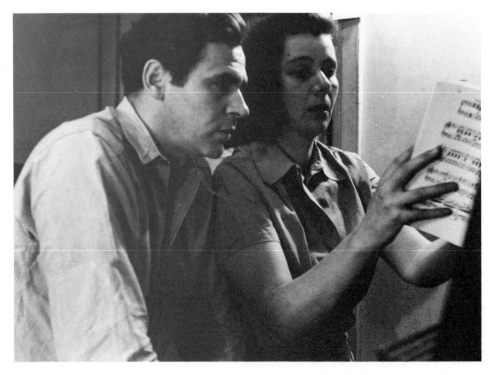

Agee holding Andrea Maria Agee, 1950.
(Photo courtesy Mia Agee)

Agee holding Julia Teresa Agee, 1947.
(Photo courtesy Mia Agee)

(Photo by Helen Levitt)

John Huston

I had written Agee a letter. He had reviewed a picture I made during the war. When I was in the army I did a picture called *The Battle of San Pietro*, which is a combat documentary. He wrote a review that was so deeply understanding and sensitive that I addressed him in a letter, one of the few times I ever did that to a critic. And he answered; he appreciated my appreciation and looked forward to a meeting sometime.

James Agee

February 21, 1948

Mr. John Huston
Warner Bros.
Burbank, California

Dear Mr. Huston:

That is true about the liabilities involved, if the critic and the criticized know each other. But to quite an extent they are involved, even seeing work of someone you don't know at all: enough so, that any critic is a fool who thinks he can be completely detached and fair— though he is also much worse than a fool if he doesn't try to come as near that as possible. But the only kinds of people I dread meeting or knowing, are those who are extemely good in their intentions but show very little ability, and those who have real but very small, or uneven, or confused or declining ability. The mixtures of sympathy and distaste in those cases are made much harder to try to handle, if you know the people personally. But I feel no such uneasiness in the thought of meeting people whose ability I consistently and greatly respect, as I do yours. I realize I'm liable through my enthusiasm and satisfaction not to be at the same time as sharp for drawbacks as a good reviewer ought to be: but at least I know I need have no scruples about trying to be: also, with any of the work you like best you automatically are applying the hardest standards you know of, according to which it would be impossible as well as unfair to review most things. Yes, I would like very much to have a drink. If you'd like to, I hope you'll come down for an evening. My wife also likes your work a great deal, and would I'm sure enjoy meeting you again. (She talked with you once under her office name of Mia Fritsch, working for *Fortune*, when you were making *Let There Be Light*.)

Thank you very much for your letter.

John Huston

And then he got in touch with me after I was out of the army and had made a couple of films, notably *The Treasure of Sierra Madre*. And he said he'd like to come out and do an article. So we went on a shooting trip up in Idaho, and Jim had a big time on that. I became very fond of him—liked him very much. He didn't shoot, didn't shoot a gun, but he enjoyed it enormously.

He said at the time he wanted to leave reviewing, to leave criticism. And he had a deep and abiding love for motion pictures, and so I said, "How about doing a picture with me?" He said he'd like nothing better, so we collaborated on the script of the next one I did—*The African Queen*.

Mia Fritsch Agee

Jim did a script on *The Blue Hotel* and that was the basis on which Huston asked him to come out. [Huntington] Hartford bought the script and Huston was supposed to do it at some point but never did.

They hit it off very well when they met. They had similar kinds of imagination. They looked at things a great deal the same way, which made them want to work with each other on a film. Huston very much liked Jim's writing and at that point didn't want to do any more writing of his own for film, so it seemed a natural that they would work together.

He started actually on the Crane story [*The Red Badge of Courage*]. That's what they started working on first—Jim, unofficially, because he wasn't doing anything on it directly. They'd talk a lot about it and Jim was at the shootings all day. They'd watch the rushes in the evening and then they'd start shooting again the next day. They were out at Huston's ranch for most of the shooting. If you worked with Huston on a film you spent every minute with him; this was not a nine-to-five proposition.

James Agee

December 1950

Dear Father [Flye],

I'll be staying out until late January, working on a script with John Huston, *The African Queen*. If everything works out right, it could be a wonderful movie; if much works out wrong, it could be lousier than most. I haven't read a book since I've been out here. I see a lot of people and like most of them. Compared with most of the intellectual literary acquaintances I avoid in New York, they are mostly very warm-hearted, outgoing, kind, happy and unpretentious, the nicest kind of company, except at home with best friends.

John Huston

We went up to a place in Santa Barbara, a resort hotel, and stayed there and wrote a script. We worked hard. And we were also on a health regimen. We'd get up early in the morning, play a couple sets of tennis, have breakfast, then go to work, work through until lunchtime, lay off for a couple of hours, then work again for two or three hours, and another two or three sets of tennis, dinner, and after dinner we'd work. I would write a section and give it to Jim. Jim would write and give it to me. Most of what Jim wrote stayed as Jim had written it, and most of what I wrote, Jim rewrote. So the collaboration was a one-sided one, and much to my benefit. I had great admiration for Jim's writing and he justified it in every way.

We agreed about so many things, we would speak in a kind of code right away. And I loved talking to Jim: He was a great man with words, but not to listen to himself. Jim's one of those people that, I don't think, ever heard the sound of his own voice. But he loved talking.

Jim was forever bringing more pages. He was doing an enormous amount of work, and I didn't see how he managed to turn so much work

Agee in Hollywood. (Photo by Florence Homolka)

(Photo by Florence Homolka)

(Photo by Florence Homolka)

out, and then I discovered that he was working at night and getting very little sleep. He was a night man, and a lot of what he was doing in the daytime was to please me. So we cut down on that. But it wasn't all that long afterward that he had his first heart attack. We had just finished the script.

Mia Fritsch Agee

So they were out on this ranch in California, and, as I say, Huston was in a reform stage, and slept, and ate, and played tennis, and so on. He was really building himself up. Jim thought all this was very fine except that when Huston went to bed at eleven o'clock or something reasonable like that, then Jim started to work. So then he'd work all night through and then at six-thirty or so he'd start playing tennis, and that was too much.

John Huston

I remember after he had his heart attack we were alone in a room, the curtains drawn, and so on. This was two or three days after the heart attack. And Jim said, "Could I have a cigarette, John?" and I said, "No, Jim, I can't do that. You know you're not supposed to have cigarettes now." And Jim said, "I'm not going to change my way of life because of this." I said, "Well, you have a lot of friends that wish you would." And he said, "Give me a cigarette," and I said, "No, Jim, it wouldn't be fair to the doctor." He thought about that, nodded, and didn't ask anymore.

Mia Fritsch Agee

He wrote an incredible amount. You say, "Why didn't they get finished?" Well, there are lots of reasons why they didn't get finished, among other things because he worked on too many things simultaneously. I know there's the idea, generally, that there's so little he wrote. But actually, if you put it all together and consider all forms of

(Photo by Florence Homolka)

writing—what he did for *Time*, what he did for *The Nation*, what he did for film, et cetera, et cetera—when you put it all together it's a hell of a lot of writing.

James Agee

April 6, 1951
Los Angeles, California

Dear Aunt Mossie [Agee's father's sister]

All you say about divorce and remarriage I agree with and am especially glad of—Grandmother had the same humane understanding and good sense about the whole thing and that's one of the main ways it seems to me the human race is divided—between those who would kill others (or themselves) for the sake of a principle—and those who know that people and their needs and their well-being mean a lot more than any principle. . . .

I enjoy movie-writing much more than magazine work, and hope I can do a lot of it—but I also very much hope not to move out here. I imagine it's middle age coming on, but I no longer feel at home in new places. The places I feel really at home are Tennessee (and more or less, anywhere in the South) and on our place up in the country in New York State, and out here I just feel as if I were treading water. But I do have a nice time here, aside from that, because I like the work and the people and have made some good friends. . . .

Considering that I might be dead or an invalid, it doesn't seem like much to have to cut far down on smoking and drinking and exertion— yet I'm finding it hard to do. Always having had a great deal of energy and good health, I have no habit of taking care of myself—so if I just try to be "moderate" it's very easy to forget. . . . On the tragic scale of some friends of mine, who are really wrecked by it, I'm not an alcoholic, but I am certainly a naturally hard drinker. After one drink it's very hard not to take another, and after three it is even harder not to take three more, and after that I'm apt to lose count and stop caring how much I drink. So my ration is two on ordinary days and four on special occasions, and

Hollywood, 1951. (Photo by Florence Homolka)

except for one drunken night, I've held to this all right for the past few weeks.

I'm awfully glad you like the book. I like things in it but in many ways feel badly about it, for by now I can see so many ways I could have made it so much better. —Please remember me with love to Ida and Ruth, and very much love to yourself. I hope I'll see you before long.

—Jim

Mia Fritsch Agee

Jim had met Chaplin at a press interview after *Monsieur Verdoux* in New York, where Chaplin was very much attacked. Jim came to his defense at the meeting because he was outraged at the way Chaplin was treated and the kinds of questions he was asked. So he came up with some perfunctory questions of his own which stopped the show. He met Chaplin at that meeting—at least to talk to him for five minutes.

When Jim went out to Hollywood, they were good friends. He absolutely adored Chaplin. That year I was out, we spent quite a lot of time with him. He was an enormously stimulating person. I mean he was interested in so many different things—very articulate and very warm. Once he trusted you, or once he accepted you, he was very open, very free, and very, very nice to be around. He and Jim set each other off in terms of the kinds of things they talked about since they were largely interested in very similar things, you know, that sort of pleasure when somebody else's mind clicks with yours, and you can really have a kind of exchange and bounce the ball around. You can't do that with most people; it is a great pleasure, you know, if you happen to hit it.

He had all sorts of ideas of films that he wanted Chaplin to make. And then also, Chaplin used him as a critic, though he never paid any attention to any criticism. But he was always very interested and he made Jim write out what he thought. He was then shooting *Limelight*, and Jim was at all the shootings. So he'd have Jim tell him what he thought about various scenes. And Jim would, of course, tell him very honestly. Of course, Chaplin never paid attention to what he said. But it didn't matter. As far as their relationship was concerned, this was perfectly all right. This was a sort of dance that you went through.

James Agee

Dear Father Flye:

I've probably spent thirty or fifty evenings talking alone most of the night with Chaplin, and he has been very open and intimate. Very interesting, to put it mildly, to see what a man of real genius is really like. Few, if any mysteries or surprises about that. The roots are emotion and intuitiveness; the chief necessity is discipline. Well, I'm not getting a bit.

Mia Fritsch Agee

He had an idea which I think would have been a very good film; a film that Chaplin should make with a return of The Tramp as one of the few, if not the only, survivor in a postatomic world. And Chaplin liked the idea very much. If that's the last person in the world, then it's also, in a way, the first person, so then the circle closes and there are lots of possibilities. It might have been complicated for him because of the sound when, after all, the films with The Tramp were all silent. But then, you see, you could conceivably, at least in large parts, have justified a silent film, which is what Jim was after anyway. In the postatomic explosion world, this would probably go quite well, since of course there wasn't anybody for him to talk with. There were no sounds. What would there be? So it would have had to go into pantomime.

He was so involved in the visual scenes of what the world would be like. Just think what you'd do with a place like New York City without a soul in it. The images are so fantastic that he never got as far as worrying about the plot.

He started writing an outline, not a real script. All I remember is the shadows that had been burned into rock by some atomic explosion. I don't think he worked out more than a third of the film, if that much. He was very interested in it for a while, but he never did it due to a combination of things. Chaplin was working on *Limelight*. They had started talking about it before, but he had already done most of the work for *Limelight* so he obviously had to follow through and finish it. They

James and Mia Agee with Charles and Oona Chaplin,
the Stork Club. (Photo courtesy Mia Agee)

were still talking about possibly doing a film together. Then he [Chaplin] went to Europe, and of course he didn't know he wasn't going to come back until the last minute. In fact, he didn't know that until after he had left on the boat. He had only left with the idea of a vacation and showing his children Europe. And, of course, he never came back. He wasn't a citizen and the government wouldn't give him a reentry permit.

Robert Saudek

The Abe Lincoln series was an integral part of the "Omnibus" television series, which had all manner of things in it. Jim and I, as students, had both had a special interest in Lincoln. He was particularly struck by Walt Whitman's poetry and by that aspect of Lincoln which was dark and moody, as Jim was some of the time.

Many years later, when "Omnibus" was on the air, which would have been the early fifties, Jim had had a heart attack and was on the coast in a hospital. At that time, I thought we would like to do a series of films on Lincoln, and I called Jim in the hospital from New York. I think he was probably very pleased to know that he did have a professional life ahead of him, that someone did want him to work. I can believe he did feel that way about it because it was, I'm sure, lonely and frustrating for him in the circumstances in which he found himself. So we talked about it and he said yes, he would like very much to do it. He began to make notes while he was in the hospital. Then he came back to New York and we met and talked about it a great deal, and finally began to shape five films.

Jim appeared in one of the films as Jack Kelso, a poet, a real character in Lincoln's early years. He sat over the Sangamon River, which was precisely the river which Lincoln lived on in those years, and he recited one of Shakespeare's sonnets, as he lifted a jug of liquor over his shoulder and took a swig from time to time.

Jim, I think, was something of a frustrated actor, and played more than once, as you may know, in other films. He had all the enthusiasm and bravura of a good actor, and perhaps, less of the control that a good

actor would have to have. It was interesting that he chose the role that he did, which I'm sure he wrote for himself. It was really Agee; Jack Kelso's character was unknown to anyone. Agee built himself into it in that fashion, which we all thought was marvelous. It is a very believable, very credible Agee, really. It's a very moving performance. If one were to see it isolated and not know that it was part of a story of Abraham Lincoln I think one would know that it was Agee.

John Huston

I loved Jim's looks. Of course, Jim didn't give a damn about his looks. It might have been the same shirt I first met him in he wore the last time I saw him, or the same necktie. His clothes just assumed the shape of his body, and one felt that if they were put on a hanger you might mistake them for Jim himself.

And as far as his physical self was concerned—teeth missing, they'd been knocked out, and it never occurred to him to have new ones put in. I guess people had remarked on this to Jim and had said "Why don't you, Jim?" so often that when he laughed he'd hold his hand up. But going to a dentist would be going too far. He didn't take care of himself at all.

He wouldn't have been Jim if he'd been one to protect himself and look after his health, and do what was best for his body and his interests. Jim lived regardless of consequences of that kind. He was beyond taking care of himself.

Robert Fitzgerald

Jim, of course, famously disregarded all precautions of the kind that are regarded as wise. He never went to the dentist; when his teeth were rotten, they fell out. He never wore overshoes or anything like that—he was soaked in winter. And all this he seemed to get away with because of what *seemed* his great ruggedness. He was not, in fact, as rugged as he looked.

We talked one day about "keeping in shape" and I quoted Remy de Gourmont, saying that a writer wrote with his whole body, and of course this was enthusiastically accepted by Jim, who did everything with everything he had—body, blood, and bones went into everything. My inference in that was "better take care of that and hold on to it; if you're going to write with your body then keep your body in shape." I don't think that this was the inference that he drew.

Mia Fritsch Agee

He was a man of excesses and of extremes, and that is inevitably to some extent self-destructive. He was a slightly larger-than-life-size person, so he tended to overdo whatever he was interested in doing at all. Anything. Friends: by spending much too much time with them, *always* being available, *always* being there when anybody wanted him. It's not a mode by which you get very much work done. He would fit his work in or just sit up all night, not doing some relatively simple things to take care of himself—like seeing to it that he got even five hours of sleep a night.

Jim certainly had very little to do with organized religions. He had an organized church in back of him because he was brought up Episcopalian and his mother was a very religious person. But in his adult life he had very little to do with any specific church. It depends on what your definition of religion is. If you see it as a kind of a search, Jim certainly had it; but I'm not sure most people would agree with that definition. He had a religious nerve which many people don't have. I don't know how to say how that was expressed since it's really a mode of mind or a way of looking or a way of approaching things, rather than something you write down as a set of rules.

He had been in and out of analysis; he went for a time in the forties to a Jungian, largely out of curiosity, and because he liked the person he was seeing. I gave him a Rorschach test for a birthday present and I'll never forget—the poor woman went absolutely out of her mind. She said it took her all day to give him the readings, while it normally takes about twenty minutes, or half an hour at the most. But, he had enormous and endless free associations; it was just like Niagara Falls. It just never stopped; it just went on and on and on and on.

Father Flye

He had a very strong constitution; and he was well built and strong and vigorous and muscular. But a person has to take some care of himself. I wrote him once or twice about those things. I thought he could sleep better if he'd look up a physical director or gym courses such as are advertised. A good trainer will give you a recipe and you could find that you could get into a regime where you could sleep better and get more rest when you needed rest and exercise when you needed exercise. But he would have probably thought, Well, that's a good suggestion, and never carry it out.

David McDowell

He was generally writing Father Flye when he was down, and frequently when he was half in the bag. He was a night worker you know; he was an insomniac. That is the greatest tragedy in his life I think, the fact that he couldn't sleep—I think that eventually killed him. He cut way down on smoking—he never gave it up. He cut way down on drinking, but he still had this incredible thing of not being able to get to sleep until dawn, and there's one thing that a heart patient simply must have and that's rest. After he had written or talked or whatever he could do, and everybody else had gone to sleep on him, he'd wander around trying to find somebody who was still up. Then he would sit down, incapable of doing any real creative stuff, and write a letter, more often than not, in depression. You see, in the letters to Father Flye there's almost no discussion of some of the things that were key to Agee. Music is hardly mentioned. There is very little stuff on the movies. There's far more in there about his personal things because Father Flye was constantly writing him and asking, "I'm worried about you—how are you feeling? I don't think you are taking care of yourself," and so on. And he would try to reassure Father Flye sometimes and sometimes he didn't reassure him

Agee during filming of The African Queen, *Hollywood,
1951. (Photo by Florence Homolka)*

at all because he said, "I feel like hell, I feel I'm dying." And you know, that gives a pretty grim, almost hypochondriacal sense about Agee as a person, and he wasn't like that at all.

Mia Fritsch Agee

I mean he was constitutionally unable to seriously consider moderation, or not doing what he wanted to do, so this never really dawned on him. I mean he never thought of himself as an invalid in the first place. Temperamentally, he was totally unsuited to that. He would take a few stabs at it like smoking less or drinking less, but it would never last very long because he would simply forget it.

John Huston

I never saw Jim drunk by the way. I know he did get drunk on a few occasions. And once drunk I understand he was deeply offended by some remark which I'm sure was offensive, and took a man who was quite powerful himself and "stove him agin the wall." One of the few times that Jim ever displayed temper of that kind. But Jim was utterly congenial, and in some way inspired the hope on your part that the world would come to terms with itself.

There'd be an argument, even a disagreement. Jim would say one thing and somebody else would say the opposite. But Jim would find some way of bringing him around into agreement. It would be a misunderstanding, but presently they would be in perfect agreement. Or at least, the other man would think so. And Jim would think so, too, yes. There was a kind of genius—a dialectic that would discover its point, its purpose. In those long nights of talks you felt that in these conversations there was an attempt on Jim's part to reconcile divergent opinions, find a common ground. And when he did, why it was cause for celebration.

James Agee

[From a spoken letter to Mrs. Flye, 1953]

This is an unwritten letter. The effort is to just speak it into a microphone. This was an idea of Father Flye's who has for the summer a recording machine. I like the idea very much, but it puts a tremendous burden of ingenuity and improvisatory power upon the speaker, and that may leave me rather helpless at times.

The job I was doing was one I believe would interest you. And I wish that we could spend an evening and go over the screenplay I wrote about it. It was about Paul Gauguin. And my sense of how to write about him was not as the criminal romantic that he's often set up, but as a man whose vocation was like a lure, set out by God, and everyone has a different lure, and his was a very deep passion for painting.

And that it take him the rest of his life from when he first felt that vocation very deeply, to find that it was not the real thing even, but only the lure—and that all it was trying to teach him was to be as absolutely faithful to his own soul and his own being as he could, and that he find out the price of that as he went along. And there's a good deal of it that I feel very well about, and that I wish I could show you.

Robert Fitzgerald

When you come right down to it, the religious sense of life is at the heart of all of Agee's work. The sense that we do live in a mysterious, very mysterious universe, that human life is constantly under the shadow of death. These overpowering convictions stand behind everything that he did. "Blessed are the merciful" would be one of the things most obviously on his mind, first and last, because that is what he most constantly felt—the need for mercy toward people who suffer. Walker Evans, who was not at all Christian, used to say that Agee had a greater taste for suffering than any man since Jesus Christ. This was Evans's kind of mood and style. And Jim himself would have appreciated Walker saying that.

Father Flye

It's a religious quality. I don't quite want to say temperament. I'm not certain of just the words to use. But there are persons who have a basic outlook or feeling or reaction that I would call religious. One element, I'm sure, in it is a sense of wonder and reverence. Some people have that and some don't. There's a sentence in one of Einstein's books that I came across many, many years ago and I liked it, and I think I can quote it: "The fairest thing we can experience is the mysterious. It is the basic emotion that stands at the cradle of all science. He who has it not, who can no longer wonder, no longer feel amazement, is as good as dead." I'd say people divide in that—in that sense of mystery and wonder that I'd call a religious sense. Some people have that just naturally, and may not be professed to be religious, but they have that feeling and that leads us to the feeling of something much higher and utterly beyond us. That is, I should think it would lead us to the feeling that there must be an intelligence with things evidently planned. Heaven on earth!!! How could as complicated a thing as various material structures of the atoms, or the pollination and process of seeding of a flower, for example—how could this come in unless there was something to say "Yes, this is so," in order that such may happen. But you better look out, if you used that term "in order that." That means purpose and a plan, and a plan means a planner. But some people haven't it. They think, well, it just exists, that's all. And others are just carried away with this sense of wonder. They feel a sense of worship. Well, Jim had that strongly. He could never have been an atheist, but he would have felt that of some of the things that have been put into doctrines or dogmas—"I must say, I just don't know." But not with the feeling that "I know this is all bunk." And so I never thought of him as irreligious. I couldn't use that word in connection with him, though he had gotten away from some of the full practice of the religion in which he was brought up. But in one of his letters to me I remember he said, "Well, sometimes I think that nothing will satisfy me except a return to religion, perhaps the one I was brought up with. At other times I am equally certain that I shall not."

Of all persons I've ever known he was one who could weigh different angles from which one might view a situation, and say, "Yes, this

Father Flye in New York City, 1942.
(Photo by James Agee)

Agee in New York City, 1942. (Photo
by Father James Harold Flye)

is so, but we must take account of this other fact also." And to some persons he would be exasperating. They would think, Make up your mind and say yes, yes. And he would say, "Yes, I accept this, but on the other hand there is this that you must be thinking of also."

It was very difficult for him, if not impossible, to join something like an association, or organization, or a union, or a political party, or perhaps a church organization. He said, "Yes, I believe a good deal, but if you ask me to go one hundred percent with you, I can't do it. Sometimes I think you're wrong." So that would apply politically and economically and almost every way, as well as religiously.

James Agee

April 1954
New York

Dear Alma:

Your letter came this morning, and it was good to hear from you. . . . It brings up a lot of things which might be answered or brought up, or talked about, and I'll at least make a start at it. . . .

You speak of Joel, and his abilities, and his lack of discipline in work, and his strong feeling against leaving home for school—all entirely sympathetic and to be expected—his lack of wish to leave home. But I feel very concerned about it, particularly the disciplined work. It's perfect hell what it can play against talent; as bad or worse than rigid censorship or a rigid religion, or dipsomania, or misused sex, or extreme neurosis. In my own way, I'm a hard and in general fairly effective worker, but I'm horrified every time I reflect on the amount of life and gifts I have wasted or not used well enough, simply through some fundamental failures and lack in habits of self-discipline. Beyond the very good things I know he has, there is nothing I could more urgently wish for him, and that he gets it during these growing years, for later on it's very much harder to come by. . . .

You ask what's been going on with me, and I realize that between my, at least, infrequent correspondence and my still less frequent mailing of the letters I do write, there must be a hell of a lot of gaps left unfilled. I'll try to begin to fill in, knowing, though, that it's more than I can better than begin in one letter. . . .

You ask whether I've changed; many ways I'm not sure I know. A few I can think of: I'm so and so many years older; by which I mean simply that I've lived that much longer. The combination of aging and of living closely with children has made me a good deal more responsible than I used to be, and a good deal more skeptical of a lot of ideas about how to raise children. And both the aging and the children, plus perhaps the illness, have combined to give me an awareness of death and of the precariousness of living which has become a sort of tuning-fork resonance which pervades and gives key to a great deal of day-to-day living, and dealing with others, and thinking. . . .

Along with this, as a part of it, a certain religious sense or aliveness I've always had has probably deepened somewhat and has certainly become more calm and real, less literary—the same as with my sense of death—and probably more pervasive, though I can't imagine it at all likely that I would ever go back into any organized kind of religion. I can't accept that kind of dogma or any other kind sufficiently. Quite outside of dogma, I can't, for instance, feel in the slightest any belief in a life after death. But I do certainly believe in the existence of some kind or other of superhuman or divine consciousness, power and love. At times, this belief amounts to conviction; at others, it's about the average of the kind of agnostic who is not anti-religious. Along with this there is much that I hate about religion and how it is used against people, but though this qualifies my religious feelings it does not reduce them.

Politically, it's harder to say where I am. Again, as a briefly descriptive phrase I'd say I'm a political agnostic, but I can try to describe it a little further than that. . . . Perhaps, I could say that my political faith is in the individual and in whatever I suppose is for the concept and the growth of the individual; that I tend to be against whatever is against it and for anything that is for it. . . .

I have very little hope that the things I most value will prevail, and very little doubt that they will survive. That they will survive may not seem like enough to ask, but it seems enough to be grateful for and to pin every hope and effort on. If I try to bring it down into labels, I am non-Communist, and for that matter anti-Communist, in enough ways to make the label stick as true without for a moment being able to swallow the kind of crap which is currently run in the more fervent ends of the anti-Communist press: the idea, for instance, that all evil is embodied in Communism, or that anyone who now remains pro-Communist or neutral must be either a dupe or a criminal. I know a lot too much better than that. . . .

On the other end, I am, in the degree that I am anything positive, reluctantly positive. My rear guard action was a faith in democratic Socialism, until I became sufficiently convinced that here, too, in the conflict between liberty and security, liberty had to die, or anyhow to be hobbled beyond what I could accept or give allegiance to. . . .

There is so much that is obviously an infernal machine about free enterprise Capitalism, that I certainly can't accept that or give all allegiance to either, but I begin to have the feeling that in any alive conflict between this which I dislike wholly but which seems one fairly clear expression of what human life is about, and the general principles of democratic Socialism (which is also an expression of what life is or hopes to be, and which I merely doubt and regret) there may still be possibly a working and flexible balance to be struck or anyhow approximated. It won't be one at best that I personally care much for, but it may in its continuous conflict, hold better promise of life—that is of relative life and relative liberty—for more people than any other prospect I can see, but again I doubt it. I think most likely, that the irreversible and many-sided effects of applied science, whatever happens in political difference and victory and defeat, will mean the end of all of us as I care most for, except in the very defeated but surviving minority. I feel that essentially I am of a dying and almost extinct species which may never become quite extinct and which almost certainly won't come to power again—and I'm not sure that matters—for centuries; a kind of semi-civilized descendant of the Greeks, through the Renaissance. I feel that my kind has had its time, and that the future—and for that matter the present—is in other hands, and on the whole I want no part of it, but believe in continuing to do my best for and in what I value, supposing that the best I can do is to help keep alive and to help to pass on dying and discredited ideas which I value above all others.

David McDowell

He had bought that broken-down farm up in Hillsdale, New York, roughly two hundred acres. It was not an active farm; it had been at one time but it had long been marginal. We went up there, oh, perhaps close to a half a dozen times, sometimes with Mia and the children and with my wife, and during that summer and into the next year, from time to time he read me sections of *A Death in the Family*. And, to the best of my memory, it was basically the way it was at the end. Though I think that the whole composition of *A Death in the Family* was basically something that started back as early as the Exeter years.

I saw him at a party on May 13, 1955. He was getting ready to go up to Hillsdale, where he felt that within a month or two months he could finish *A Death in the Family*. The end was already written. I don't know what he would have done in the way of transitions between the two levels of time in it: one, when he was the baby and before the birth of Emma, and then the other time section where Emma's in there. I made no changes in the manuscript—there were twenty or so miscellaneous pages that I couldn't fit anyplace. He would have added more I'm sure, but I think he would've been most concerned with working out the transitions. But basically, it was finished, and certainly the end was perfectly obvious—he clearly intended doing nothing beyond the butterfly.

His mother once told me that he had written about doing something—probably a novel but maybe a long poem—on the death of his father, as far back as when he was at Exeter, at sixteen or seventeen. *A Death in the Family* was written almost during his whole life.

A good many people feel that *A Death in the Family* is completely autobiographical. Well, the basic scene is, but there are extraordinary things in there that never happened, including one of the very best scenes in the book, the visit to Great Grandma—that is absolutely fictional. The priest who visits the house is fictional. A priest did, but he didn't resemble him at all. This is not just simply exactly everything that happened, but a very, very shrewd artist's reworking of material and changing it to fit a theme and a plot.

He was artistically one of the most generous people—reading other

people's work and he was constantly reading things to people—more so than any writer I've ever known. When he read something to them it was not to show off but to see from how they reacted, what they thought of it. And he read to me for hours and hours. He had no conception of himself as a genius, certainly. He knew he was talented; he was too shrewd an artist himself and too honest an artist to feel otherwise. Yet, I think he felt he was a failure in the sense that he really hadn't gotten things across. Toward the end of his life, none of his work was in print except anthology pieces.

James Agee

New York City
1955

Dear Father Flye:

Depending on what I turn out to be capable of, I might go to Ireland to work with Huston on Kipling's *The Man Who Would Be King*, or write a film for Williamsburg, or might finish a novel, or translate a play by Cocteau, or again, might write a movie script about Quakers during the Civil War, or might adapt a novel called *The Way West*. So I'm less at a loss for work than for choice and for time, and the question among them of money, and of what I can afford to do for little or no money.

I've been better during the past week, dropping by and large from an average twelve to seventeen attacks per day, to an average of six to eight. At moments I wonder whether those who go as I do, for a Full Life, don't get their exact reward, which is that the Full Life is full of crap. At other moments, I realize equally well that this is what life is all about. In any event, God bless you.

Father Flye

At supper time, May sixteenth, I had a telephone call from David [McDowell] telling me that Jim had died. I got a plane that evening and was in New York the next morning. Jim was the closest to me of anyone

Agee in King Street house in New York City, 1955. (Photos by Helen Levitt)

JAMES AGEE, 45, POET AND CRITIC

Ex-Film Reviewer for Time Dies—Wrote Scenarios, Novel and Narrations

James Agee, a poet, critic and sensitive writer in many media, died Monday of a heart attack, suffered while going by taxi from his Greenwich Village home, 17 King Street, to a physician's office.

Mr. Agee was 45 years old and had suffered from heart disease for the last two years.

Two years after his graduation from Harvard, Mr. Agee published his first work, a book of verse that he called "Permit Me Voyage." Archibald MacLeish, a poet of established reputation, said the young writer had a "delicate and perceptive ear." The New York Times Book Review noted "his awareness of the changing ideas of society" and his "stubborn faith in enduring values."

Similar comments followed Mr. Agee throughout his career. Mr. Agee was on the editorial staff of Fortune magazine from 1932 to 1935 and on the staff of Time from 1939 to 1948. One of his managing editors on Time called him "the finest writer Time ever had."

Interest in Films

For some years Mr. Agee wrote film criticism for Time and other magazines, including The Nation, Partisan Review, Harper's and the Forum. His interest in the film media led him to devote much of his time from 1948 onward to motion pictures.

Mr. Agee wrote and narrated the commentary for a short, independently poduced film about an underprivileged Harlem boy, called "The Quiet One." Bosley Crowther The Times motion picture critic, wrote that the "narration is beautifully simplified and phrased."

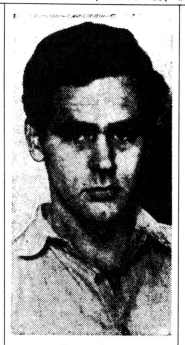

James Agee

He wrote the script for "The African Queen," which was directed by John Huston. He also wrote the script for "Night of the Hunter," an as yet unreleased film directed by Charles Laughton.

This week an Italian travel film of the South American jungles, "Green Magic," opened in New York with English narration by Mr. Agee.

Mr. Agee wrote a text-and-picture book in association with Walker Evans, the well-known photographer, about the life of sharecroppers in Alabama. This was called "Let Us Now Praise Famous Men." Many critics gave the book high praise but Ralph Thompson, writing in The New York Times, attacked it as "arrogant, mannered, precious, gross."

He published a novel in 1951 called "The Morning Watch," which The Times declared "in tone, imagery and movement * * * has something of the quality of a dark poem."

He is survived by his widow, Mia, and three children.

in the world, and I could not have had a deeper personal grief than at his death. As to the circumstances, he had felt very well the day before [Sunday]. Monday afternoon he had taken a taxi to go uptown and had a heart attack on the way. The driver went to the nearest hospital [Roosevelt], but Jim was dead.

I don't suppose he ever would have been satisfied with his life. But he did produce quite an output after all. But he would have liked to do much, much more. And to take various of those subjects and go with them. He was very much interested in human life, in human lives, in his own life. And here is the little sketch of *A Death in the Family*, that narration of a few days in a boy's life. I'm perfectly sure he would have liked to go back to the time of his great-grandparents and get all the information he could about them and then his grandparents and certainly his parents, and then about his own birth, and so on, and develop that. You could have had an autobiography of fifty volumes, I suppose.

FROM "Now as Awareness" *in* The Collected Short Prose of James Agee

(Evidently a fresh start on the autobiographical novel. No date)

Now as awareness of how much life is lost, and how little is left, becomes even more piercing, I feel also, and ever more urgently, the desire to restore, and to make a little less impermanent, such of my lost life as I can, beginning with the beginning and coming as far forward as need be. This is the simplest, most primitive of the desires which can move a writer. I hope I shall come to other things in time; in time to write them. Before I do, if I am ever to do so, I must sufficiently satisfy this first, most childlike need.

Those who have gone before, backward beyond remembrance and beyond the beginning of imagination, backward among the emergent beasts, and the blind, prescient ravenings of the youngest sea, those children of the sun, I mean, who brought forth those, who wove, spread the human net, and who brought forth me; they are fallen backward into their graves like blown wheat and are folded under the earth like babies in blankets, and they are all melted upon the mute enduring world like leaves, like wet snow; they are faint in the urgencies of my small being as stars at noon; they people the silence of my soul like bats in a cave; they lived, in their time, as I live now, each a universe within which, for a while, to die was inconceivable, and their living was as bright and brief as sparks on a chimney wall, and now they lie dead, as I shall lie; my ancestors, my veterans.

Then there are those who come within living memory: my mother's father's father, whom she revered and of whom she has told me; I think well of him, and was burdened by his name, but I never knew him; I doubt I shall ever have occasion to tell my children of him; with this generation he vanishes from the memory of the human race, and only the exceptionally good, or able, or evil survive in memory longer.

Afterword

Year after year, as I use Agee's writing in my courses and read student papers about him, I ask myself, as they do, why we are reading him—what he means to us more than a generation after his untimely death. In my lectures I try to stress his singular gifts: an expert craftsman with the English language; a voice of brave and candid dissatisfaction with the way things are—the inhumanity, the injustice, the meaness and callousness, the smugness and arrogance; a giant of a person, whose wide-ranging, restless, hungry mind crossed all sorts of boundaries and borders and passed beyond established limits; a teacher, who through poems and stories and essays made us morally uncomfortable, morally alert, a bit more morally searching; and not least, a pilgrim, ever asking whither, ever uncertain, yet ever willing and anxious to keep going on this vexing, perplexing journey that is allowed us so mysteriously, a gift we spend a lifetime trying to know what to do with.

Once, a student sent me a note after the course I taught was over. He was twenty and dying of leukemia. Still, he continued to attend lectures, read books, wrote papers, and felt it was his duty, his responsibility to himself, to "keep going as before," as he put it. In his note he had this to say about James Agee:

I expect to die in a few months. I'll be less than half as old as he was when he died. I've been reading everything of his I can get my hands on. I feel that he's the one who has the most to say to me, before I die. The reason is this: He seemed to have lived each day as if it was a gift, and as if it was his last, and he wrote that way. He makes me feel that there's reason to be proud that I'm a human being, that I can sit and read James Agee and understand what he wrote and respond to his language and his ideas. A lot of the time, after I read the newspapers or the weekly news magazines, or watch the news on television, I'm ashamed to be a human being, because of all the terrible things we do to one another. We make animals seem so civilized!

But with Agee, your faith is restored. He was such a good person; and he was such a wonderful writer. I'm sure he had his faults, like the rest of us. But he gets through to you. He reaches your heart, and he reaches your mind. A lot of people reach your heart, and a lot of intellectuals reach your mind, but to do both, to make you feel and make you think—and even to make you try to be a better person, that's a lot! To me, Agee is someone who knew what it meant to live in this crazy century. He only lived forty-five years, but he saw it all, the wars, the nuclear madness, the Depression, Hitler and Stalin. Even so, he kept his sense of humor, and he wrote those beautiful books. They tell you about yourself, because they tell you what a human being is, whether a child or a teenager, whether a poor person or a guy who tries to under-

stand poor people, those way below him on the social ladder, and with no money at all.

There was more, including a self-deprecatory apologia worthy of Agee himself. I have kept that letter tucked in a copy of *Let Us Now Praise Famous Men*—a decent, thoughtful, dying youth's homage to a writer who had a keen and abiding sense of how fragile and tentative all things are, how precious it is, this existence allowed us. James Agee was a promising poet who never became the mature lyrical and even metaphysical poet he might have been. He was a shrewd and knowing and marvelously poignant storyteller who never became the self-assured and controlled narrator of fiction he might have been. He never, that is, got far enough beyond himself and his given world—the distance a great novelist must gain on life. He was a sharp, powerful critic, of both books and films, though he never wrote long pieces of analysis and argument, as some of our finest essayists have done. He was an utterly unique and brilliant social observer; his effort to penetrate and portray the Alabama world of 1936 stands apart from the rest of the field of documentary literature—an example that gives all the rest of us pause and humbles us. He made a beginning as a movie scriptwriter, though the enormous talent, great good humor, and magical dramatic sense were already apparent. He was, not least, a letter writer. He not only corresponded with Father Flye, but with other quite special and gifted people, like Dwight Macdonald and Robert Fitzgerald. He was someone for whom friendship was fertile ground for talk—continuing, contained, highly intelligent discourse. One can imagine the different conversations his letters might have contained had he lived on into quieter, less driven, autumn years. Not least, he was a truly exceptional person, thoroughly and completely and in every aspect *sui generis*.

While we mourn what we lost by his death, we must also declare our gratitude for what was given us—a rich talent, brightly displayed, to enduring effect. The fact is that the young man dying of leukemia is not alone. He is one of thousands who have known James Agee through his work: men and women grappling hard with the moral issues of our world, men and women trying to figure out what matters, truly matters, as against the superficial things which come and go, the flashy diversions which tempt us and which help us betray ourselves.

We are left, I suspect, with Flannery O'Connor's judgment with respect to the novelist's task, not to mention that of the man or woman or child who looks upward toward the skies with hope and prayer: that the mystery of this world be deepened, always, in our contemplation—a mystery alive in each of us, and alive, too, in the memory we have of those gone. She meant that we are in constant danger of selling each other short, forgetting to notice what a miracle it can be, again and again, this "spirit become flesh"—hers, though she'd never have said so, and Lord knows, Lord yes, Lord thank you, James Agee's: a brief but stunning burst of heavenly light upon our darkness, and thereby, a search redeemed, because the cumulative moral message of his life, offered in such lively, compelling diversity, was noticed, is noticed, will continue and continue to be noticed.

The Works of James Agee

Agee on Film: Reviews and Comments, vol. 1. New York: Perigee Books, 1983. (Originally published by McDowell, Obolensky, New York, 1958.)

Agee on Film: Five Film Scripts by James Agee, vol. 2. New York: Perigee Books, 1983. (Originally published by McDowell, Obolensky, New York, 1960.)

The Collected Poems of James Agee. Edited by Robert Fitzgerald. Boston: Houghton Mifflin, 1962.

The Collected Short Prose of James Agee. Edited by Robert Fitzgerald. Boston: Houghton Mifflin, 1962.

A Death in the Family. New York: Bantam Books, 1969. (Originally published by McDowell, Obolensky, New York, 1957.)

The Letters of James Agee to Father Flye, 2d ed. Boston: Houghton Mifflin, 1971. (Originally published by George Braziller, New York, 1962.)

Let Us Now Praise Famous Men. Boston: Houghton Mifflin, 1960. (Originally published by Houghton Mifflin, Boston, 1941.)

The Morning Watch. New York: Ballantine Books, 1966. (Originally published by Houghton Mifflin, Boston, 1951.)

Permit Me Voyage. New Haven: Yale University Press, 1934.